VMware vSphere Design Essentials

Unleash the performance, availability, and workload efficiency of your virtual data center using this fast-paced guide

Puthiyavan Udayakumar

BIRMINGHAM - MUMBAI

VMware vSphere Design Essentials

First published: June 2015

Production reference: 1260615

Published by Packt Publishing Ltd.
Livery Place
35 Livery Street
Birmingham B3 2PB, UK.

ISBN 978-1-78439-004-4

www.packtpub.com

Credits

Author
Puthiyavan Udayakumar

Reviewers
Vikas Shitole
Aravind Sivaraman

Commissioning Editor
Kartikey Pandey

Acquisition Editors
Vivek Anantharaman
Hemal Desai

Content Development Editor
Siddhesh Salvi

Technical Editor
Rahul C. Shah

Copy Editors
Sonia Michelle Cheema
Stephen Copestake
Swati Priya

Project Coordinator
Kranti Berde

Proofreader
Safis Editing

Indexer
Mariammal Chettiyar

Graphics
Disha Haria

Production Coordinator
Nilesh R. Mohite

Cover Work
Nilesh R. Mohite

About the Author

Puthiyavan Udayakumar has more than 8 years of IT experience and has expertise in areas such as Citrix, VMware, Microsoft products, and Apache CloudStack. He has extensive experience in the field of designing and implementing virtualization solutions using various Citrix, VMware, and Microsoft products. He is an IBM Certified Solution Architect and a Citrix Certified Enterprise Engineer and has more than 16 certifications in infrastructure products. He has authored *Getting Started with Citrix CloudPortal*, *Getting Started with Citrix® Provisioning Services 7.0* and *VMware vSphere Network Virtualization Recipe Book*. He holds a master's degree in science with a specialization in system software from the Birla Institute of Technology and Science, Pilani. He also has a bachelor's degree in engineering from SKR Engineering College, affiliated to Anna University, and has received a national award from the Indian Society for Technical Education. He has presented various research papers that follow the IEEE pattern at more than 15 national and international conferences, including IADIS (held in Dublin, Ireland).

About the Reviewers

Vikas Shitole is a member of technical staff at VMware R&D, where he primarily contributes to the vCenter Server team. He has received the vExpert title for the years 2014 and 2015, arecognition received from the VMware community for his outstanding contributions to the virtualization & cloud computing community. Also, he is the author and owner of vThinkBeyondVM.com, a blog focused on VMware virtualization and cloud computing. He has completed his MTech in computer science from the VIT University, India, and holds VCP51, OCPJP 1.6, and MCTS certifications. He can be followed on Twitter at `@vThinkBeyondVM`.

He was the technical reviewer of *Getting started with VMware virtual SAN*, *Packt Publishing*.

Aravind Sivaraman has over 9 years of experience in the IT field. He is currently working as a solution architect, providing the consultation, design, and delivery of complex IT infrastructure based on virtualization and cloud infrastructure solutions. He holds certification from VMware, Microsoft, and Cisco and has been awarded the VMware vExpert title for the last 3 years (2013-2015). He blogs at `http://www.aravindsivaraman.com/` and can be followed on Twitter at `@ss_aravind`.

He has coauthored *VMware ESXi Cookbook* and was the technical reviewer of *Troubleshooting vSphere Storage* and *VMware vSphere Security Cookbook*, all by Packt Publishing.

www.PacktPub.com

Support files, eBooks, discount offers, and more

For support files and downloads related to your book, please visit www.PacktPub.com.

Did you know that Packt offers eBook versions of every book published, with PDF and ePub files available? You can upgrade to the eBook version at www.PacktPub.com and as a print book customer, you are entitled to a discount on the eBook copy. Get in touch with us at service@packtpub.com for more details.

At www.PacktPub.com, you can also read a collection of free technical articles, sign up for a range of free newsletters and receive exclusive discounts and offers on Packt books and eBooks.

https://www2.packtpub.com/books/subscription/packtlib

Do you need instant solutions to your IT questions? PacktLib is Packt's online digital book library. Here, you can search, access, and read Packt's entire library of books.

Why subscribe?

- Fully searchable across every book published by Packt
- Copy and paste, print, and bookmark content
- On demand and accessible via a web browser

Free access for Packt account holders

If you have an account with Packt at www.PacktPub.com, you can use this to access PacktLib today and view 9 entirely free books. Simply use your login credentials for immediate access.

Instant updates on new Packt books

Get notified! Find out when new books are published by following @PacktEnterprise on Twitter or the *Packt Enterprise* Facebook page.

Table of Contents

Preface

This book provides the framework and methodologies that need to be applied during the initial, planning, analysis, and design phase of the VMware vSphere implementation in data centers.

This book will provide readers with the design fundamentals essential for a VMware engineer and architect, even before they implement VMware vSphere in their data centers.

After reading this book from cover to cover, readers will achieve the following:

- The essentials of VMware vSphere
- The essential skills required to design VMware vSphere management layer
- The essential skills required to design VMware vSphere network and storage
- The essential skills required to design vCloud

Readers will gain a great deal of advantage from this book. They will learn how to design a virtual data center with the given requirement and the key components that will yield great success to business and IT. They will also learn how to convert the industry standards to customer-specific by following the golden principle of the best practices recommended by VMware.

Upon finishing this book, readers will have the skills required to design, build, deploy, and manage VMs in a VMware vSphere data center with VMware ESXi and VMware vCenter Server.

What this book covers

Chapter 1, Essentials of VMware vSphere, gives readers an in-depth knowledge of VMware vSphere products' benefits and architecture, and the analysis of trends and challenges faced by IT. It also covers the appropriate methods, principles, and processes that the reader will apply to design VMware vSphere on infrastructures.

Chapter 2, Designing VMware ESXi Host, Cluster, and vCenter, covers the methods for designing an ESXi Hypervisor and its inner components. This chapter also covers methods for designing for the upgradation and migration of ESX, clusters and vCenter, and highly elastic infrastructures.

Chapter 3, Designing VMware vSphere Networking, covers the the methods for analyzing the given requirements and mapping them to network possibilities. We will also cover methods for forming design blueprints for networking infrastructures that are to be considered while designing. It also covers the scenario-based learning on network designing essentials.

Chapter 4, Designing VMware vSphere Storage, covers the methods for analyzing the given requirements and mapping them to storage possibilities, and the designing blueprints for storage infrastructure. It also deals with scenario-based learning on storage design essentials and the factors to be considered while choosing the right storage.

Chapter 5, Designing VMware vRealize, covers the methods for analyzing the given requirements and mapping them to vCloud as well as forming design blueprints for the vCloud infrastructure. It also covers the factors to be considered when choosing the right vCloud.

Appendix, About VMware vSphere 6.0, covers the new features introduced into VMware vSphere 6.0. It also covers the enhancements brought into VMware vSphere 6.0 in the network, storage, management, and availability areas, and shows a brief feature comparison between VMware vSphere 5.5 and VMware vSphere 6.0.

What you need for this book

You will need to have a basic understanding of virtualization, and some hands-on experience with either a VMware vSphere product or any other server virtualization product.

Go to `https://my.vmware.com/web/vmware/downloads` and download the following products:

- VMware vCloud Suite
- VMware vSphere
- VMware vRealize Suite

Who this book is for

This book is for VMware beginners, engineers, SMEs, and architects.

Conventions

In this book, you will find a number of text styles that distinguish between different kinds of information. Here are some examples of these styles and an explanation of their meaning.

Code words in text, database table names, folder names, filenames, file extensions, pathnames, dummy URLs, user input, and Twitter handles are shown as follows: "The `esxcli` command-line tool."

A block of code is set as follows:

```
#esxcfg-module -g bnx2x#esxcfg-module-gs2io (for the Neterion)
#esxcfg-module-g ixgbe (for the Intel)
```

Any command-line input or output is written as follows:

```
vicfg-vswitch
```

New terms and **important words** are shown in bold. Words that you see on the screen, for example, in menus or dialog boxes, appear in the text like this: "Though there are huge enhancements in vSphere 5.1 and as shared storage is no longer an obligation for vMotion, **Distributed Resource Scheduler** (**DRS**) will not use VMs local storage."

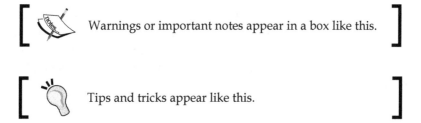

[Warnings or important notes appear in a box like this.]

[Tips and tricks appear like this.]

Reader feedback

Feedback from our readers is always welcome. Let us know what you think about this book—what you liked or disliked. Reader feedback is important for us as it helps us develop titles that you will really get the most out of.

To send us general feedback, simply e-mail feedback@packtpub.com, and mention the book's title in the subject of your message.

If there is a topic that you have expertise in and you are interested in either writing or contributing to a book, see our author guide at www.packtpub.com/authors.

Customer support

Now that you are the proud owner of a Packt book, we have a number of things to help you to get the most from your purchase.

Errata

Although we have taken every care to ensure the accuracy of our content, mistakes do happen. If you find a mistake in one of our books—maybe a mistake in the text or the code—we would be grateful if you could report this to us. By doing so, you can save other readers from frustration and help us improve subsequent versions of this book. If you find any errata, please report them by visiting http://www.packtpub.com/submit-errata, selecting your book, clicking on the **Errata Submission Form** link, and entering the details of your errata. Once your errata are verified, your submission will be accepted and the errata will be uploaded to our website or added to any list of existing errata under the Errata section of that title.

To view the previously submitted errata, go to https://www.packtpub.com/books/content/support and enter the name of the book in the search field. The required information will appear under the **Errata** section.

Piracy

Piracy of copyrighted material on the Internet is an ongoing problem across all media. At Packt, we take the protection of our copyright and licenses very seriously. If you come across any illegal copies of our works in any form on the Internet, please provide us with the location address or website name immediately so that we can pursue a remedy.

Please contact us at copyright@packtpub.com with a link to the suspected pirated material.

We appreciate your help in protecting our authors and our ability to bring you valuable content.

Questions

If you have a problem with any aspect of this book, you can contact us at questions@packtpub.com, and we will do our best to address the problem.

1
Essentials of VMware vSphere

Thanks for choosing *VMware vSphere Design Essentials*, your companion in learning the fundamentals of designing VMware vSphere. We understand your mission to learn, apply, and reap the benefits of virtualization and to design VMware vSphere to its fullest extent using this book. Let's get started learning about VMware vSphere and its essentials.

VMware vSphere is a product developed by VMware, Inc. The company is located at Palo Alto, California, USA, and was started in 1998. It offers virtualization, cloud software, and services. VMware vSphere is a product that aims to provide x86 virtualization to renovate datacenters into streamlined cloud computing infrastructures, which in turn enables IT organizations to deliver consistent and elastic IT services.

vSphere virtualizes physical hardware and converts one single physical system into multiple VMs; thereby VMware vSphere reduces the space, cost, and complexity of managing systems in a datacenter. This book is not only for VMware architects but also for people who use vSphere on a daily basis. This book will help you understand how vSphere is designed and will help you to design your virtual infrastructure using VMware vSphere to its best potential. Also this book will help you to improve your skills; you will become well versed in designing best practices.

Designing VMware vSphere infrastructure will be a multipart subject. In this chapter, we'll provide an introduction to the VMware vSphere landscape, the design of vSphere itself, challenges and obstacles that were caused by virtual infrastructure due to poor design, and the way to overcome those challenges with structured principles and processes.

In this chapter, you will learn the following topics:

- Introduction to the VMware vSphere landscape
- Designing VMware vSphere
- Challenges and obstacles faced with the virtual infrastructure
- Designs that will accelerate solutions to resolve real-world obstacles
- Values and procedures that need to be followed while designing VMware vSphere

Introducing the VMware vSphere landscape

VMware vSphere is built for infrastructure virtualization. The benefits of this product are as follows:

- Virtualizing x86 systems
- Virtualizing networks
- Virtualizing storage
- Built-in security and High Availability
- Automated monitoring

The VMware vSphere landscape is formed by the following mandatory components. If the infrastructure is designed without any one of these components, it will result in issues such as poor performance, poor user experience, and applications not working. Let's take a look at the components of vSphere in the following table:

Components	Description
ESXi	This provides a virtualization layer that contains computing, network, and storage resources of the ESXi host into several VMs. We will see more information on designing the management layer in the upcoming chapters.
Management layer	This is nothing but a vCenter that provides a layer as a vital administration point for ESXi hosts associated on your network. We will see more information on designing the management layer in the upcoming chapters.

Components	Description
vCompute	This is nothing but a collection of virtual memory, virtual CPUs, and virtual network interface cards; all these components form vCompute
	We will see more information on designing the management layer in the upcoming chapters.
vNetwork	This links VMs to one other within ESXi host, establish the communication between VMs virtual NIC to the physical network, and along with that also provides a communication chancel services for VMkernel services (including NFS, iSCSI, vMotion)
	We will see more information on designing vNetwork in the upcoming chapters.
vStorage	This is nothing but an application interface layer, which in turn provides an abstraction layer to manage and modify physical storage during implementation.
	We will see more information on designing vStorage in upcoming sections in this chapter.
Database	This acts a data management point to organize all the configuration data for the VMware vSphere infrastructure.
	We will see more information on designing databases in upcoming sections in this chapter.

Designing these components is highly critical for virtualization success. The following diagram illustrates the associations within each component:

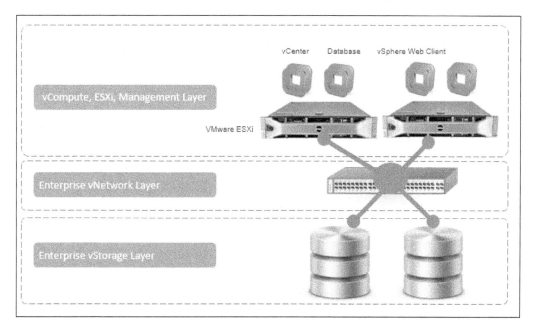

You need to have understood component associations within VMware vSphere. As the next step, start designing essentials before we jump into designing each component. Let's get started with understanding the essentials of designing VMware vSphere. Designing is nothing but assembling and integrating VMware vSphere infrastructure components together to form the baseline for a virtualized datacenter. It has the following benefits:

- Saves power consumption
- Decreases the datacenter footprint and helps towards server consolidation
- Fastest server provisioning
- On-demand QA lab environments
- Decreases hardware vendor dependency
- Aids to move to the cloud
- Greater savings and affordability
- Superior security and High Availability

Designing VMware vSphere

Architecture design principles are usually developed by the VMware architect in concurrence with the enterprise CIO, Infrastructure Architecture Board, and other key business stakeholders.

From my experience, I would always urge you to have frequent meetings to observe functional requirements as much as possible. This will create a win-win situation for you and the requestor and show you how to get things done. Please follow your own approach, if it works.

Architecture design principles should be developed by the overall IT principles specific to the customer's demands, if they exist. If not, they should be selected to ensure positioning of IT strategies in line with business approaches. In nutshell, architect should aim to form an effective architecture principles that fulfills the infrastructure demands, following are high level principles that should be followed across any design:

- Design mission and plans
- Design strategic initiatives
- External influencing factors

When you release a design to the customer, keep in mind that the design must have the following principles:

- Understandable and robust
- Complete and consistent
- Stable and capable of accepting continuous requirement-based changes
- Rational and controlled technical diversity

Without the preceding principles, I wouldn't recommend you to release your design to anyone even for peer review.

For every design, irrespective of the product that you are about to design, try the following approach; it should work well but if required I would recommend you make changes to the approach.

The following approach is called **PPP**, which will focus on people's requirements, the product's capacity, and the process that helps to bridge the gap between the product capacity and people requirements:

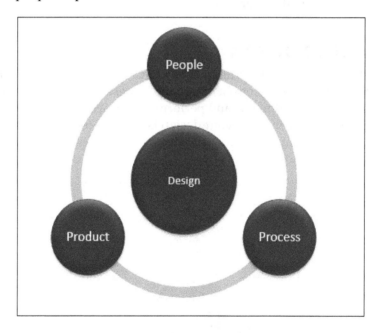

The preceding diagram illustrates three entities that should be considered while designing VMware vSphere infrastructure.

Please keep in mind that your design is just a product designed by a process that is based on people's needs.

In the end, using this unified framework will aid you in getting rid of any known risks and its implications.

Functional requirements should be meaningful; while designing, please make sure there is a meaning to your design. Selecting VMware vSphere from other competitors should not be a random pick, you should always list the benefits of VMware vSphere. Some of them are as follows:

- Server consolidation and easy hardware changes
- Dynamic provisioning of resources to your compute node
- Templates, snapshots, vMotion, DRS, DPM, High Availability, fault tolerance, auto monitoring, and solutions for warnings and alerts
- Virtual Desktop Infrastructure (VDI), building a disaster recovery site, fast deployments, and decommissions

The PPP framework

Let's explore the components that integrate to form the PPP framework. Always keep in mind that the design should consist of people, processes, and products that meet the unified functional requirements and performance benchmark. Always expect the unexpected. Without these metrics, your design is incomplete; PPP always retains its own decision metrics. What does it do, who does it, and how is it done? We will see the answers in the following diagrams:

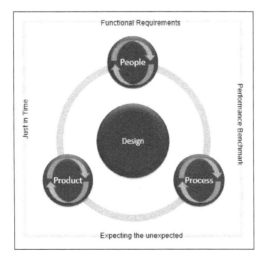

The PPP Framework helps you to get started with requirements gathering, design vision, business architecture, infrastructure architecture, opportunities and solutions, migration planning, fixing the tone for implementing and design governance. The following table illustrates the essentials of the three-dimensional approach and the basic questions that are required to be answered before you start designing or documenting about designing, which will in turn help to understand the real requirements for a specific design:

Phase	Description	Key components
Product	Results of what?	In what hardware will the VM reside?
		What kind of CPU is required?
		What is the quantity of CPU, RAM, storage per host/VM?
		What kind of storage is required?
		What kind of network is required?
		What are the standard applications that need to be rolled out?
		What kind of power and cooling are required?
		How much rack and floor space is demanded?
People	Results of who?	Who is responsible for infrastructure provisioning?
		Who manages the data center and supplies the power?
		Who is responsible for implementation of the hardware and software patches?
		Who is responsible for storage and back up?
		Who is responsible for security and hardware support?
Process	Results of how?	How should we manage the virtual infrastructure?
		How should we manage hosted VMs?
		How should we provision VM on demand?
		How should a DR site be active during a primary site failure?
		How should we provision storage and backup?
		How should we take snapshots of VMs?
		How should we monitor and perform periodic health checks?

Before we start to apply the PPP framework on VMware vSphere, we will discuss the list of challenges and encounters faced on the virtual infrastructure.

List of challenges and encounters faced on the virtual infrastructure

In this section, we will see a list of challenges and encounters faced with virtual infrastructure due to the simple reason that we fail to capture the functional and non-functional demands of business users, or do not understand the fit-for-purpose concept:

- **Resource Estimate Misfire**: If you underestimate the amount of memory required up-front, you could change the number of VMs you attempt to run on the VMware ESXi host hardware.

- **Resource unavailability**: Without capacity management and configuration management, you cannot create dozens or hundreds of VMs on a single host. Some of the VMs could consume all resources, leaving other VMs unknown.

- **High utilization**: An army of VMs can also throw workflows off-balance due to the complexities they can bring to provisioning and operational tasks.

- **Business continuity**: Unlike a PC environment, VMs cannot be backed up to an actual hard drive. This is why 80 percent of IT professionals believe that virtualization backup is a great technological challenge.

- **Security**: More than six out of ten IT professionals believe that data protection is a top technological challenge.

- **Backward compatibility**: This is especially challenging for certain apps and systems that are dependent on legacy systems.

- **Monitoring performance**: Unlike physical servers, you cannot monitor the performance of VMs with common hardware resources such as CPU, memory, and storage.

- **Restriction of licensing**: Before you install software on virtual machines, read the license agreements; they might not support this; hence, by hosting on VMs, you might violate the agreement.

- **Sizing the database and mailbox**: Proper sizing of databases and mailboxes is really critical to the organization's communication systems and for applications.

- **Poor design of storage and network**: A poor storage design or a networking design resulting from a failure to properly involve the required teams within an organization is a **sure-fire** way to ensure that this design isn't successful.

Planning, designing, and positioning a virtualization-based infrastructure are really difficult tasks. There are sizable technical hurdles for administrators to jump, but often it's the challenge of getting everyone to pull in the same direction that ultimately slows a virtualization rollout. Let's explore the top 10 considerations that should be considered before starting to design a VMware virtualization and the best time to start. According to VMware experts, the right stage to start considering, is the beginning, which leads on to the following questions:

- Why is the customer seeking to implement VMware vSphere?
- What applications does the customer plan to deploy?
- What objective does the customer hope to reach with the help of a VMware vSphere deployment?
- What are the existing problems, business or technical, that the customer is trying to resolve?

Requirement gathering and **documenting** are the driving factors for virtualization; the objectives, problems and needs of the customer should be the first task to undertake before we can start designing. This is the beginning and translates into what we have called the design factors—requirements, constraints, risks, and assumptions. They are crucial to the success of any vSphere design. In the next section, you will learn the ways in which we can overcome the challenges and enforcements.

Designing accelerates the solution that resolves real-world obstacles

This section provides a step by step sequence and activity that is required to be followed in order to design a virtualization; this is a completely elastic method that best fulfills your infrastructure demands. The steps are obtainable in an ordered sequence as per the following diagram:

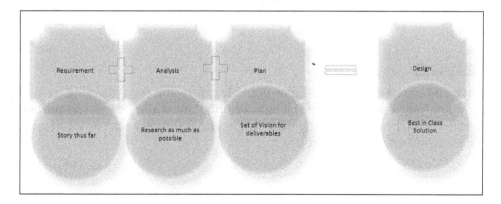

Requirements

It's really difficult to build a virtual infrastructure if you don't know the target or requirements. **Elicitation** is the step where the requirements are first gathered from the customer. Many practices are available for gathering requirements. Each has a certain value in certain situations; you need manifold techniques to gain a complete picture from various sets of clients and stakeholders. Here's a look at some of the approaches you can take:

- One-on-one meeting with IT leaders and top management sponsors for the project
- Team meetings with the current team responsible for managing technical operations
- Facilitated sessions, prototyping, initial engagement surveys, use cases, following people around, **Request for Proposals** (**RFPs**), brainstorming

Finally, at the end of requirement gathering, conduct workshops with all these reviews, lastly look for room for improvement. If all stakeholders in a session try to appraise the value and cost for each demands, at last artifacts becomes much more effective and cost-valuable. Hence, schedule periodic meetings to review and agree requirements:

 Documentation helps to identify the current state of infrastructure and helps to identify inputs for our next stage in the analysis.

Analysis

Research and collect data facts as far as possible before you start planning for design; since the analysis or research must be lightweight, it must also be less scrupulous. Best results come from considering user insights from the very start as input and giving the result to the design process.

In the early stages of the process, the discovery stage will help you identify new breaks and will describe the design in brief. VMware vExperts advise re-iterative ESXi and VM configuration testing before it is rolled out to the **Proof of Concept (POC)**. In turn, this will help to inform decisions from the design phase to the final implementation. A usability problem can be corrected more swiftly and with less cost if it is identified at the design stage itself rather than at the support stage.

We will use the 4D-stage analysis process to display how we can fit in all the stages:

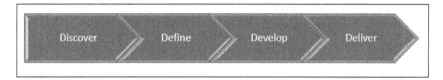

The preceding 4D stage analysis, as explained in the following table, aligns to the method that is required to be adopted in each stage:

Phase	Description	Methods
Discover	Engage with the business and observe the requirements, in the context of demand and services.	Cognitive Map
Define	Interpret requirements, rationalize, and verify business demands. This is a key input for the design for it to proceed to further stages.	Task and gap analysis
Develop	Key metrics need to be finalized with the help of cognitive map and analysis output, because the method we develop will be followed during the design phase.	Prototyping
Deliver	Evaluate the prototype with the business to verify and refine the requirements and align the design towards an agreed solution.	Quantitative and qualitative

With this approach, we will be able to gain an insight into requirements and the output of this phase is an input to the planning phase. As the next step, let's learn about planning and its implications to the design phase.

Planning

The design considerations we made in final steps may make us to change the decisions which we made in the earlier steps, due to various thought clashes. Every alert challenges the potential requirement gathering, planning, and design, which will be a great challenge throughout the project planning.

We will come to design phase which meets best of our requirements, only after iterating through the stages as many times as required to include all of the thoughts within the manuscript. The following diagram illustrates the key technical metrics that are required to be a part of your planning technical artifacts:

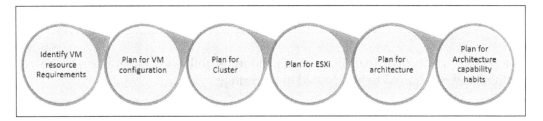

Each phase of planning and its mission is listed in the following table:

Phases of planning	Key objectives
Identify VM resource requirements	Mission 1: Determine the workload resource requirements
	Mission 2: Define the workload characterizations
Plan for VM configuration	Mission 1: Define the compute configuration
	Mission 2: Define the network configuration
	Mission 3: Define the storage configuration
	Mission 4: Define the VM availability strategy
	Mission 5: Define the VM types
Plan for cluster	Mission 1: Define the physical locations
	Mission 2: Define the ESXi host cluster
	Mission 3: Determine the cluster ESXi host members
Plan for ESXi hosts	Mission 1: Define the compute configuration
	Mission 2: Define the network configuration
	Mission 3: Define the storage configuration
	Mission 4: Define the server virtualization host scale
	Mission 5: Define the server virtualization host availability strategy

Phases of planning	Key objectives
Plan for DRS and DPM	Mission 1: Define the priority configuration
	Mission 2: Define the algorithm and calculate it
	Mission 3: Define the threshold configuration
	Mission 4: Define the balanced average CPU loads or reservations
	Mission 5: Define the balanced average memory loads or reservations
	Mission 6: Define resource pool reservations
	Mission 7: Define an affinity rule
Plan for HA and FT	Mission 1: Define monitoring mechanisms for physical servers and VMs
	Mission 2: Define server failure detection
	Mission 3: Define migration and restart of VM Priority from failed ESXi host
	Mission 4: Define the **vLockstep technology** for FT
	Mission 5: Define the transparent failover
	Mission 6: Define the component failures
Plan for VMware architecture	Mission 1: Define the maintenance domains
	Mission 2: Define the physical fault domains Mission 3: Define the reserve capacity
Plan for architecture capability habits	Mission 1: Define the original SLA factors for storage and VMs
	Mission 2: Define the original costs for storage and VMs

If you're looking for a tool that can do this, then the best tool to use (and one that VMware recommends) is **VMware Capacity Planner**. It is the right thing to start with.

VMware Capacity Planner is a capacity planning product that gathers comprehensive resource consumption data in assorted IT environments and associates it to industry standard position data to provide analysis and decision support modeling. The following are the key benefits of the product:

- Increased efficiency with server union and volume optimization
- Reduced complication through IT calibration and hardware restraint
- Improved expectations with capacity consumption trends and virtualization targets

The output of data gathering from the requirements, analysis, and planning phases is a design phase input. This is really a key factor for your success. In the next section, let's explore the key requirements for designing in general and then we will map that to the streamlined process and principles.

Designing

Design essentials are what this book is all about. Let's get started by looking at the fundamentals. Any design, irrespective of the platform, should be enabled with factors such as balance, proximity, alignment, repetition, contrast, and space. These factors, in turn, should focus on the following:

- Identifying design thoughts and encounters
- Describing where to start with customers
- Describing procedures for dealing with decision architects
- Identifying if you've achieved design acceptance
- Identifying what your framework should include
- Identifying the phases of design
- Identifying the risks associated with the discovery phase
- Identifying the best practices that can fit the customer's needs.
- Identifying the method that is capable of either scale-out or horizontal scaling

The preceding components will help you to attain the following deliverables that will help you to build the right solution document for small, medium, and enterprise businesses:

- Design component and logical view
- Design references architecture
- Design sizing and scalability capacity
- Design of ESXi host
- Design of VMware vSphere Management Layer
- Design of VMware vSphere Network Layer
- Design of VMware vSphere Storage Layer

The values and procedures to be followed while designing VMware vSphere

Designing VMware vSphere is really challenging; to avoid any bottleneck, we need to learn and understand how it is really done by experienced architects and VMware itself. In the following section, we will discuss the values and procedures that need to be followed while designing VMware vSphere.

As you are aware, inputs for each design have to come from the PPP framework in order to achieve the desired success, including decision-influencing factors. This helps us to satisfy the functional requirements and performance benchmarks.

Start your design by focusing on the business drivers, and not the product features. The products could be the best in the world, but no good for your use case irrespective of any conditions. For example, if you have been asked to design your VMware vSphere-based Hadoop clusters, the driving factors for your design decision would not include fault tolerance. However, for a business-critical application, fault tolerance will be vital and, if that business-critical application needs more than one CPU, then we would not be able to use VMware vSphere Fault Tolerance to continue its uptime. On the design document, the feature looks good, but it doesn't work in the real infrastructure. The following diagram illustrates values of virtualization and its subcomponents:

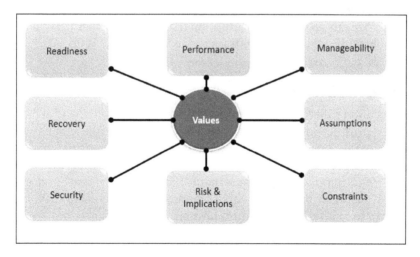

Readiness

As we make decisions that will form a VMware vSphere design, one value to be considered most is **readiness**.

Readiness is all about integrating different components together: uptime and system reliability, downtime, redundancy, and resiliency. In a nutshell, a mechanism that avoids crashes and maintains performance.

Values should have a close relationship with each other. With regard to the PPP framework of design, the value of readiness typically has the greatest effect on product decisions.

In some cases, the functional requirements explicitly call for readiness; for example, a functional and performance requirement may demand that the vSphere design must provide 99 percent readiness to meet any demand. In this case, readiness is explicitly noted by the requirement gathering and therefore must be incorporated into the design.

In some other cases, the functional requirements may not explicitly state readiness demands at 99 percent. In these cases, the designer should include an appropriate level of availability as per the projected target state.

To accommodate both cases in the design document, always come up with an assumption section. An assumption section can offer justification for the vSphere designer's decisions within the broader business framework of functional performance requirements, design consideration, and constraints. When readiness isn't explicitly stated, the designer can provide an assumption that the infrastructure will be made as ready as possible within the cost limitations of the statement of work.

Performance

Performance is often called for in the performance requirements, and it can affect decisions in the product and people phases. For the product phase, it can affect all manner of design decisions, starting from the type of the server's hardware to the kind of network storage devices planned. With regard to the performance demand, it's mostly seen as a **Service Level Agreement (SLA)** that expresses performance metrics, such as response times per request, transactions per second in the network, and the capacity to handle the maximum number of users.

If there is no performance requirement explicitly defined, the designer of a vSphere infrastructure should consider **performance** as a key component for its design decisions.

The KA key stage is to review and agree the performance metrics and make sure they have been documented on a **low-level design**, as well as ensuring that the specified components are validated against the gathered requirements. The key components that need to be considered and validated are as follows:

- For hardware or CPU, the designer should consider options such as Hardware Assisted Computing Virtualization, Hardware Assisted I/O Memory Managed units Virtualization and Hardware Assisted Memory Managed units Virtualization.

- For Network adapters, the designer should consider the following; such as Checksum Offload, **TCP Segmentation Offload** (**TSO**), the ability to handle high-memory DMA (that is, 64-bit DMA addresses), the ability to handle multiple Scatter Gather elements per Tx frame, **Jumbo frames** (**JF**), and **Large Receive Offload** (**LRO**). When using VXLAN, the NICs should support offload of encapsulated packets.

- For memory, the designer should consider factors such as NUMA, paging size, memory overhead, and memory swapping.

- For storage, the designer should consider options such as **vSphere Flash Read Cache** (**vFRC**), **VMware vStorage APIs for Array Integration** (**VAAI**), LUN Access Methods, virtual disk modes, linked clones, and virtual disk types.

- For network, the designer should consider the following such as **Network I/O Control** (**NetIOC**), DirectPath I/O, **Single Root I/O Virtualization** (**SR-IOV**), SplitRx Mode, and Virtual Network Interrupt Coalescing.

Manageability

The designer should consider that the management pane has a key component that should be documented in a design document. **Manageability** is a key factor that works on support and operations. As a part of the support, managing infrastructure is most essential; hence, manageability is integrated from various factors:

- Reachability from one infrastructure environment to another environment, from one location to another location

- Usability, scalability, and interoperability

- Access, manipulation, scripting, and automating common administrative tasks

- Obtaining statistics from guest operating systems

- Extending the vSphere Client GUI to vCLI

- Monitoring mechanisms to manage server hardware and storage

- Performance monitoring mechanisms and obtaining historical data

Recovery

Recovery after a disaster is a key design principle that should be considered. With traditional disaster recovery procedures, the IT team have to identify a way for budgets to support the solution and make decisions about exactly which systems will not be sheltered. This process made ease via virtualization and along with a arrival of disaster recovery offerings via private and public clouds. Resiliency services and business continuity services are now ease for administer to manage, in turn makes huge disaster recovery protection for all applications.

To protect critical data and systems, only a few tools are available in the market today, especially to query real-time data replication and failover. It is critical for vSphere designers to understand that these tools are required for the appropriate infrastructure, and it is very important for designers to know exactly which systems and data need to be protected along with the type of protection that they are demanded, defining the metrics become one of the main design essentials for vSphere.

To start with, the first key metric is the **Recovery Point Objective (RPO)**. For any data protection tool, RPO defines how much data could be lost in the recovery procedure. In case a single disk drive in the RAID 5 array undergoes failure, then there is no associated data loss. This is called as RPO of zero. At worst case scenario is that the entire disk in an array undergoes failure. In this situation, if a business demands data restoration from the last good known tape backup, the RPO time for this would be 12 to 24 hours. Essential of defining RPO of VMs is highly demanding, along with an integrating of tools in the design document.

The next serious metric is **Recovery Time Objective (RTO)**. Used along with RPO, RTO measures the time taken for the entire recovery process up until the time where the end user can reconnect to their applications.

For example, if a production server fails and reaches a state where the server should be reimaged using the same tape backup solution, the RTO could be hours or days. This is will depend on time taken to repair the existing hardware or build the new hardware, followed by installing the host, guest OS and followed by applications deployment time . Hence, integrating this information on your design document is essential.

Once recovery objectives such as RPO and RTO have been finalized, most organization discovers that a traditional tape backup alone is not enough to meet their objective of high availability for many critical applications, Therefore, many organization will implement integration of different solutions such as data replication and application high availability attached with guest OS virtualization.

Security

Security is yet another key principle that has to be incorporated into virtualization design. VMware has its own product for security — **VMware vShield Endpoint (VSE)**. VSE offers endpoint protection by command of magnitude and divests anti-threat agent processing inside VMs that reside on ESXi and safe virtual appliance brought by VMware partners. VSE improves amalgamation ratios, performance, rationalizes antivirus deployment, monitoring for threats, and make sure compliance by logging antivirus and anti-malware activities which are accomplished in the virtual infrastructure.

Virtualization security is a key component of design. While the IT team needs to implements its own security practices and security governance in the phase of virtualization, the clear impact is that security can be really advantageous. Virtualization improves security by assembly it more fluid and context-aware solution. Which means security is more precise to manage, and cost effective to deploy than traditional security software.

Virtualization security empowers datacenter admins with the authority of automation on provision VMs. These VMs are fully wrapped with security policies that follow desktops when users move across from one system to another system.

With the accurate processes and products, virtualization has the authority to make datacenters even more secure; hence they identify the right tools to protect VMware vSphere-based virtualizations.

Assumptions

Assumptions should be an important section in the design document; without the assumption section, the planning phase cannot be driven forward. Factors that need to be considered by designers are the following:

- The existing infrastructure that can be used for the virtualization project
- Application virtualization consolidation and compatibility assessment
- List of firewall rules in place
- Trained VMware-Certified resources to deploy the solution and support it further
- Equipment that will be presented at a certain date
- The organization has satisfactory network bandwidth
- Server hardware that has to be separated between DMZ and internal servers
- Identify suitable best practices associated with a proposed design

- Subordinate a role to the material that needs to be composed
- Stakeholders that will make a decision in the next meeting
- In scope and out of scope that has to be reviewed and agreed on between the project sponsor and project supplier

If you design your capacity in such a way that your business is going to grow by 20 percent yearly, this growth will apply linearly to the ingesting of the available capacity in the datacenter. This can be categorized under assumptions.

Constraints

Constraints are a key principle that should be considered on design essentials. This section will impose obstacles and limit your design decision; it can be a technical limitation, the actual cost of the project, or the choice of vendors. Here are some examples of factors that limit the design:

- The project has to be finished in a very limited period
- The project requires infrastructure to meet the timeline
- The project budget is very limited
- Skilled resources to execute the design are very limited
- Any vendor support needs for apps, servers, storage, and networks are limited
- Any other factors that are affecting the design decision

If you purchased a SAN 3 years ago for a file server consolidation project, you plan to use it for a virtualization project, and you do not find any information about those devices, this can be categorized under the constraints section and it is really a critical component for the project execution phase.

Risk

Risk management is a key principle that is required to be considered while designing VMware vSphere infrastructure. Identifying the risk factor very early will help you to identify and highlight problems hiding inside your virtualization design effort:

- The major risk listed in the virtualization project is whether the project will be delivered on time and on budget
- Availability of technically skilled resources to complete the project on time
- Not enough network bandwidth to handle the initial load
- Isolating the infrastructure form development, pre-production to production

For example, you might be in a situation where the IT Management does not provide the required approval for changing the network core to increase iSCSI traffic. This can be characterized under risks on your design principles.

There are eight values of design as an outcome of design decisions. There are multiple ways to fulfill the functional and performance requirements, but a vSphere designer must evaluate each of the following against these eight values:

- Does the choice positively or negatively impact the readiness of the design?
- What about the design's manageability or performance?
- What about recoverability and security?
- What about risks, constraints, and assumption associated with it?

These principles provide generic guidance and direction on the best way to meet the functional and performance requirements for a particular design.

Before we wrap up this chapter, we will look at a final section on the process of designing VMware vSphere with its essentials.

Procedures to be followed while designing VMware vSphere

Now that we've discussed the PPP framework of design and the value of design, it's time to discuss the procedure of design. In this section, we'll start with how we go about creating a VMware vSphere design. The following procedure illustrates the various processes that are required to be followed while creating a VMware vSphere design:

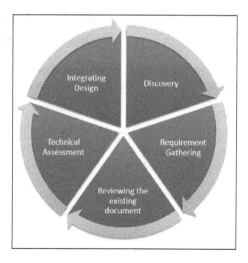

Discovery

Discovery is the key, and first stage of your design. This element will help you to get the following questions answered:

- What are the needs of business users?
- Which of the services currently meet those needs?
- How are users performing?
- What industrial or policy-linked restraints might there be?

Before you start building a design you need to build up a blueprint of what the context for that design is. This means lots of end user research, and a close assessment of current infrastructure and policies, ethics, and business needs.

Requirement gathering

Let's get started with requirement gathering, which is an important part of any IT virtualization project. Understanding what those requirements will bring, is success to virtualization project. Shockingly it's an part that is frequently given far too little courtesy.

Numerous designs start with the greenest list of demands, where some of via verse, for those we need focus and avoid these bottleneck ,by producing a document of requirements. This requirement document will acts as bible for design phase. It will, in turn, provide the following benefits as well:

- A brief functional requirement for design purposes.
- A statement of key objectives—a *prime points* condition
- A description of the infrastructure in which the virtualization will work
- Information on major design constraints to meet the requirements

The context on the statement of requirements should be stable. Architect should not allow state of changes, which will relatively slow down the phase of design and so forth.

Upon finalization of statement of requirements, make sure the business and respective stakeholders sign up and agrees to it. Technical artifacts expectation should inline to statement of requirements. No deviation should be entrained.

Here are well-known rules that will you help you successfully complete your requirement gathering:

- Never assume what we have is what our client wants for
- Involve the appropriate stakeholder right from beginning
- Review, define and agree the scope of work for the virtualization
- Make sure that the functional, nonfunctional and operational requirements are specific, measurable and realistic
- Create a crystal-clear, detailed requirement document and share it with all the stakeholders to gain their confidence on the virtualization project
- Demonstrate your understanding of the business requirements with all stakeholders (again and again)

Reviewing the existing document

Today, many organizations invest time and effort in building their requirements prior to engaging suppliers and consultants. Organizations implementing VMware vSphere have fully documented their functional requirements. This documentation often has outlines stating the organization objective.

For example, perhaps the enterprise is implementing virtualization as part of a VDI/Shared Desktop virtualization initiative. In that case, some of the functional and performances requirement of the VMware vSphere environment can be a show-stopper. In your VDI project, an initial requirement may be that the vSphere infrastructure should automatically restart VMs in the event of an ESXi host failure. The moment you read the statement, you may want to use vSphere High Availability on your design document in order to meet the given performance requirement. Since you have planned to use VMware vSphere High Availability, implementation of clusters is required. This, in turn means you have to set up redundant management connections that distress the networking and storage design and so forth.

Another case. Let's say an enterprise is migrating to a new datacenter and a team that has compiled the number of applications that have to be migrated. From that documentation, we can better understand the application requirements and identify the functional and performance requirements required to be supported by the virtual infrastructure that is intended to be designed. Possibly, the application dashboard documentation indicates that the IOPS profile is mainly writes instead of reads. This is a key element for designing the storage.

Though reviewing the existing documentation will be helpful, it's unlikely that you'll find all the information required for your design. But it is really worthwhile to spend time in identifying what is already available; it will save your time bridging the gap.

Technical assessment

Technical assessment is a critical step between the planning and design of a virtualization project. It has three important modules—infrastructure assessment, business assessment, and operational assessment. The goal of the technical assessment is to inventory current infrastructure and identify virtualization candidates.

The key deliverables of this assessment will be as follows:

- Baseline the list of servers, that are ideal candidates for virtualization
- Baseline performance and utilization, which is very much essential for capacity planning

Data collection does not have the arrangement required for the virtual server farm design. Inventory data may encompass fault values and performance reports may have wrong data, because the monitored server was shut down or not reachable via the network. Moreover, performance reports extracted from servers having disparate configurations cannot be equated unless data is standardized. Indeed, we cannot compare processor utilization reports for servers with different types of processor.

This phase is predominantly interesting when the server landscape whose data is being analyzed contains a number of servers. For each server, many data facts are available, requirements will streamline the metrics that are required to be considered; however, for the designer it is worth considering the following tools for **capacity planning** and utilization measurements:

- VMware Capacity Planner
- Countless community-supplied health-check scripts
- CiRBA and NetIQ PlateSpin Recon

After you've gathered the information required to determine the design's functional requirements, it's then required to assess the current infrastructure. Assessing the infrastructure fixes a couple of gaps and, to do that, use the gap analysis as per the customer's demand.

Design integration

Design integration is essential for the successful design of VMware vSphere. Integration of design can happen only if factors such as **data architecture**, **business architecture**, **application architecture**, and **technology architecture** are put together, as illustrated in the following diagram:

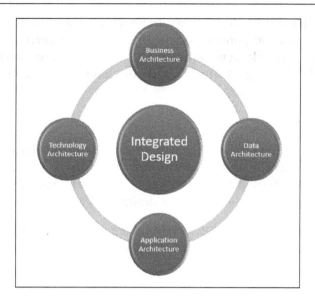

To build this type of architecture, it is always recommended to get hold of TOGAF, DMM, UML, BPMN, or any of the Enterprise Architecture frameworks to build the design:

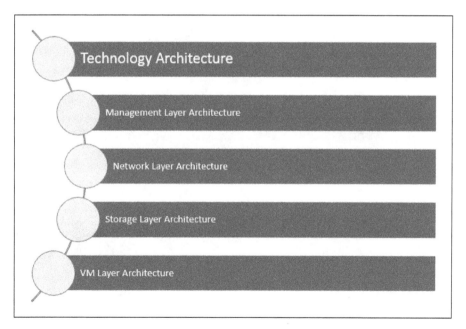

To be specific, with regard to **technology architecture**, always remember VMware vSphere should have a component model with components such as **management layer architecture**, **network layer architecture**, and **storage layer architecture**. Furthermore, it should integrate further with the cloud and SOA on demand.

Summary

In this chapter, we discussed the VMware vSphere landscape, designing VMware vSphere, and a list of challenges and encounters faced on the virtual infrastructure. Designing accelerates the solutions that resolve real-world obstacles, values, and procedures that need to be followed while designing VMware vSphere.

In the next chapter, you will learn about designing essentials for the management layer, which is, designing the VMware ESXi host, cluster, and vCenter.

2
Designing VMware ESXi Host, Cluster, and vCenter

The core elements that are responsible for the success of virtualizing our datacenter start with accurate design of ESXi and vCenter. VMware ESXi is a host OS, installed on bare metal, which is a driving factor for virtual datacenters and the cloud. VMware's ESXi hypervisors have changed a lot over the years, and the foundation of the enterprise contribution has undergone a structured transition phase.

There are a plenty of implementation options for ESXi deployment that tell us about product growth and maturity. We'll compare the choices, looking at the returns from each implementation to decide which one will be more suitable for different environments. An enterprise can now rollout ESXi in a straightforward manner and manage it constantly with policy management. In this chapter, we'll discuss the essential configurations that are required in VMware vSphere design and how to effectively design the management layer. The heart of any moral vSphere infrastructure is a strong ESXi design.

In this chapter, you will learn about the following topics:

- Design essentials for ESXi
- Designing ESXi
- Design configurations for ESXi
- Design considerations for ESXi with industry inputs
- Design essentials for upgrading ESXi
- Design essentials for migrating ESXi
- Designing essentials for the management layer
- Design decisions for the management layer
- Design considerations for the management layer with industry inputs

Design essentials for ESXi

VMware ESXi is the primary component in the VMware integrated environment. ESXi (short for Elasticity Sky X), which was formerly known as ESX and GSX, is a world-class, Type 1 hypervisor developed by VMware for implementing virtual datacenters. As a Type 1 hypervisor, ESXi is not an application—it is an OS that integrates vital OS components such as a kernel.

ESXi 5.5.0 Update 2 is the latest version and has updated drivers. It is available for public download and the following table shows the release history:

Date of Release	Name of the Release	Version	Build
December 2, 2014	ESXi550-201412001	ESXi 5.5 Express Patch 5	2302651
October 15, 2014	ESXi550-201410001	ESXi 5.5 Patch 3	2143827
September 9, 2014	VMware ESXi 5.5 Update 2	ESXi 5.5 Update 2	2068190
July 1, 2014	ESXi550-201407001	ESXi 5.5 Patch 2	1892794
June 10, 2014	ESXi550-201406001	ESXi 5.5 Express Patch 4	1881737
April 19, 2014	ESXi550-201404020	ESXi 5.5 Express Patch 3	1746974
April 19, 2014	ESXi550-201404001	ESXi 5.5 Update 1a	1746018
March 11, 2014	VMware ESXi 5.5.1 Driver Rollup		1636597
March 11, 2014	VMware ESXi 5.5 Update 1	ESXi 5.5 Update 1	1623387
December 22, 2013	ESXi550-201312001	ESXi 5.5 Patch 1	1474528
November 25, 2013	vSAN Beta Refresh		1439689
September 22, 2013	VMware ESXi 5.5	ESXi 5.5 GA	1331820

After Version 4.1, VMware released another version named ESXi. ESXi replaces **Service Console**, which is nothing but an elementary OS, with a more tightly integrated OS.

The decision to Service Console fundamentally changed what was conceivable with VMware's hypervisor. VMware ESXi demands a much smaller server footprint, so the hypervisor consumes fewer host resources to perform essentially the same functions that were performed by ESX—this is a great consolidation. ESXi also offers reduced disk utilization—whether it is OS or application, data that is consumed from local disk, or booting from a SAN disk.

The best advantage of ESXi is reduced base code, which is good in terms of security. Previous versions of ESX were shipped and downloadable with a file size of 2 GB, whereas the present ESXi version is 125 MB. It's easy to see that less code implies fewer security requirements as there is a smaller attack vector. The ESX Service Console provides additional software security, which ESXi avoids.

ESXi patches are released less frequently and are easy to apply across virtual datacenters; this massively reduces the administrative burden from a management standpoint. This is another great advantage of ESXi.

Designing ESXi

The VMware ESXi design comprises the fundamental OS and processes that run on top of ESXi, and it is called **VMkernel**. VMkernel runs all processes on ESXi, including ESXi agents, management software, as well as virtual machines. ESXi gains control over hardware devices on the physical servers and manages resources for the virtual machines. The main processes that route on top of the ESXi VMkernel are as follows:

- **Direct Console User Interface (DCUI)**
- **Virtual Machine Monitor (VMM)**
- Several agents used to enable high-level VMware infrastructure management from remote applications
- **Common Information Model (CIM)**

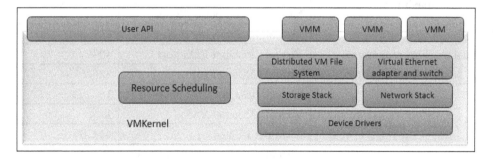

VMkernel is a POSIX-like OS developed by VMware and provides functionalities similar to other OS', such as control, process creation, process threads, signals, and filesystems. ESXi is designed precisely to support multiple VMs and provide core functionalities such as resource scheduling, I/O stacks, device drivers, and so on.

VMware ESXi was restructured to permit VMware consumers to scale out through a hypervisor that is more parallel to a hardware server. The vision was a base OS that is capable of autoconfiguring, receiving its settings remotely, and running from memory without disks. However, it's also an OS that's flexible enough to be installed on hard disks along with a locally saved state and user-defined settings for smaller, ready-to-use installations that don't require additional infrastructure.

Removing the VMware Service Console obviously has a great impact. A number of services and agents that were installed by default had to be rethought. The familiar command-line interface with its entree to management, troubleshooting, and configuration tools is swapped in ESXi, which is Linux-styled third-party agents for backups, hardware monitoring, and so on must be provisioned in different ways.

Design configurations for ESXi

In this section, you will see the key configurations that are required while designing VMware ESXi. All of the VMware ESXi hosts should be identical in terms of hardware specifications and should be built and configured reliably, to diminish the amount of operational effort involved with patch management, and to provide a building block solution. The following table illustrates the maximum configuration required while designing ESXi on your infrastructure:

Item	Designed to support	Max supported
Host CPU maximums	Logical CPUs per ESXi host	320
	NUMA Nodes per ESXi host	16
Virtual machine maximums	Virtual machines per ESXi host	512
	Virtual CPUs per ESXi host	4096
	Virtual CPUs per core	321
Fault Tolerance maximums	Virtual disks per ESXi host	16
	Virtual CPUs per VM	1
	RAM per FT VM	64 GB
	Virtual machines per ESXi host	4
Memory	RAM per ESXi host	4 TB
	Number of swap files per VM	1
Virtual Disks	Virtual Disks per ESXi host	2048

Item	Designed to support	Max supported
ISCSI Physical	LUNs per ESXi host	256
	Qlogic 1 GB iSCSI HBA initiator ports per ESXi host	4
	Broadcom 1 GB iSCSI HBA initiator ports per ESXi host	4
	Broadcom 10 GB iSCSI HBA initiator ports per ESXi host	4
	NICs that can be associated with software iSCSI stack per ESXi host	8
	Number of total paths per ESXi host	1024
	Number of paths to a LUN (software iSCSI and hardware iSCSI) per ESXi host	8
	Qlogic iSCSI: dynamic targets per adapter port per ESXi host	64
	Qlogic iSCSI: static targets per adapter port per ESXi host	62
	Broadcom 1 GB iSCSI HBA targets per adapter port per ESXi host	641
	Broadcom 10 GB iSCSI HBA targets per adapter port per ESXi host	128
	Software iSCSI targets per ESXi host	2561
NAS	NFS mounts per ESXi host	256
	LUNs per ESXi host	256
	LUN size	64 TB
	LUN ID	255
	Number of paths to a LUN	32
	Number of total paths on an ESXi host	1024
	Number of HBAs of any type	8
	HBA ports	16
	Targets per HBA	256

Item	Designed to support	Max supported
Common VFS	Volume size	64 TB
	Volumes per host	256
	Hosts per volume	64
	Powered on virtual machines per VMFS volume	2048
	Concurrent vMotion operations per VMFS volume	128
Physical NICs	1,000 1 Gb Ethernet ports (Intel PCI-e)	24
	igb 1 Gb Ethernet ports (Intel)	16
	tg3 1 Gb Ethernet ports (Broadcom)	32
	bnx2 1 Gb Ethernet ports (Broadcom)	16
	nx_nic 10 Gb Ethernet ports (NetXen)	8
	be2net 10 Gb Ethernet ports (Server engines)	8
	ixgbe 10 Gb Ethernet ports (Intel)	8
	bnx2x 10 Gb Ethernet ports (Broadcom)	8
	Combination of 10 Gb and 1Gb Ethernet ports	8 10 Gb and 4 1 Gb ports
	mlx4_en 40 GB Ethernet Ports (Mellanox)	4
VMDirectPath limits	VMDirectPath PCI/PCIe devices per host	8
	SR-IOV Number of virtual functions	642
	SR-IOV Number of 10 GB pNICs	8
	VMDirectPath PCI/PCIe devices per virtual machine	43

Item	Designed to support	Max supported
vSphere Standard and Distributed Switch	Total virtual network switch ports per host (VDS and VSS Ports)	4096
	Maximum active ports per host (VDS and VSS)	1016
	Virtual network switch creation ports per standard switch	4088
	Port groups per standard switch	512
	Static/Dynamic port groups per distributed switch	6500
	Ephemeral port groups per distributed switch	1016
	Ports per distributed switch	60000
	Distributed virtual network switch ports per vCenter	60000
	Static/dynamic port groups per vCenter	10000
	Ephemeral port groups per vCenter	1016
	Distributed switches per vCenter	128
	Distributed switches per host	16
	VSS port groups per host	1000
	LACP - LAGs per host	64
	LACP - uplink ports per LAG (Team)	32
	Hosts per distributed switch	1000
	NetIOC resource pools per vDS	64
	Link aggregation groups per vDS	64
Cluster (all clusters including HA and DRS)	Hosts per cluster	32
	Virtual machines per cluster	4000
	Virtual machines per host	512
	Powered-on virtual machine config files per data store in an HA cluster	2048

Item	Designed to support	Max supported
Resource Pool	Resource pools per host	1600
	Children per resource pool	1024
	Resource pool tree depth	82
	Resource pools per cluster	1600

Key design considerations for ESXi

In this section, the following are the most important considerations for your VMware ESXi design:

- Consider using VMware Capacity Planner to investigate the performance and usage of prevailing servers; this will help you to identity the requirements for planning.

- Consider eliminating inconsistency and achieving a controllable and manageable infrastructure by homogenizing the physical alignment of the ESXi hosts.

- Never design ESXi without a remote management console such as DRAC and ILO.

- Ensure that `syslog` is properly set up for your virtual infrastructure and log files are offloaded to non-virtual infrastructures.

- Consult your server vendor on proper memory DIMM size, placement, and type to get optimal performance. While other configurations may work, they can greatly impact memory performance.

- Ensure you choose the right hardware for the ESXi host, while aligning the functional requirements with a workload that has a baseline and performance that has a benchmark.

- Ensure higher density and consolidation are maintained in the design, always scale up the ESXi hosts; this strategy will in turn get the best RTO scales out of our distributed architecture.

- While designing, it is worth taking into consideration CPU scheduling for larger VMs, NUMA node size, and the balance between CPU and RAM to avoid underperformance. This will in turn provide sufficient I/O and network throughput for the VM.

- In your design, if you have planned to deploy SSD in the ESXi host, make sure you have enough data facts with respect to read/write performance. In today's market, most SSDs are heavily read-biased and hence worth considering in your design. Factors that need to be considered are peak network bandwidth requirements for NICs and PCI Bus. If sizing ESXi host falls under the scope of work, then give more importance to CPU, memory, network and storage bandwidth as well.

- Ensure your design has sufficient ESXi hosts to bring them into line with a scale out practice to increase DRS cluster productivity while consuming sufficient ESXi hosts for our workloads, in order to get optimal performance.

- Ensure in your design that sizing and scaling your virtual infrastructure are given more importance; continuously study using local SSD drives for local caching solutions such as vFlash Read Cache, PernixData, or any other solution of your choice for ESXi hosts.

- Ensure in your design that you are sizing your VMware ESXi hosts and consider having a lighter ESXi host instead of having more, smaller ESXi hosts; this will in turn bring more benefit in CapEx and OpEx, as well reducing the datacenter footprint.

- Size ESXi host CPU and RAM keeping the following things in mind—20 percent headroom for spikes and business peaks, VMkernel overhead, planned and unplanned downtimes, and future business growth.

Designing an ESXi scenario

Let's apply what we have learnt so far in designing ESXi 5.5 in the following scenario. Let's start with hardware merchant for our design is Dell. In this scenario, the Dell PowerEdge R715 server has been chosen as the hardware for designing and implementing VMware ESXi 5.5. The configuration and assembly process for each system should be homogeneous, with all components installed identically for all VMware ESXi 5.5 hosts. Homogenize not only the model but also the physical configuration of the VMware ESXi 5.5 hosts, to provide a simple and supportable infrastructure by eliminating unevenness. The specifications and configuration for this hardware platform are detailed in the following table:

Attributes	Modules
Vendor	Dell
Model	PowerEdge R715
Number of CPU sockets	4
Number of CPU cores	16

Attributes	Modules
Processor speed	2.3 GHz
Number of network adaptor ports	8
Network adaptor vendor(s)	Broadcom/Intel
Network adaptor model(s)	2x Broadcom 5709C dual-port onboard
Network adaptor speed	2x Intel Gigabit ET dual-port Gigabit
Installation destination	Dual SD card
VMware ESXi server version	VMware ESXi 5.5 server; build: latest

With the preceding configuration, let's start designing. The first step is to configure the **Domain Name Service** (**DNS**) for all of the VMware ESXi hosts that are required; they must be able to resolve short names and **Fully Qualified Domain Names** (**FQDN**) using forward and reverse lookup from all server and client machines that require access to VMware ESXi.

The next step is to configure **Network Time Protocol** (**NTP**). It must be configured on each ESXi host and should be configured to share the same time source as the VMware vCenter Server to ensure consistency across VMware vSphere solutions.

At this moment, VMware ESXi 5.5 offers four different solutions—local disk, USB/SD, booting from SAN, stateless booting of ESXi. In case your infrastructure requirements gathering states that we need to use stateless disk, plan your rollouts with minimal associated CapEx and OpEx. VMware provides solution to deploy ESXi on SD cards, because it will permit a cost-saving migration to stateless when required.

While installing VMware ESXi, consider the auto-configuration phase; a 4 GB VFAT scratch partition is created if a partition is not present on another disk. In this scenario, SD cards are used as the installation endpoint and will not permit the creation of a scratch partition. Creating a shared volume is suggested by industry experts. That will hold the scratch partition for all VMWare ESXi hosts in an exceptional against per-server folder. We are using one of the NFS data stores in this scenario.

For our scenario, let's consider using a minimum of four racks for the 20 hosts and layering the VMware ESXi hosts across the racks as depicted in the following diagram.

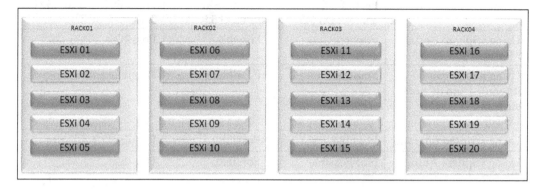

Wiring considerations for our scenario are redundant power and four power distribution units for racks, each connected to separate legs of a distribution panel or isolated on separate panels. Here, the assumption is that the distribution panels are in turn isolated and connected to different continuous power supplies.

Layering the VMware ESXi hosts across the accessible racks diminishes the impact of a single point of failure.

Design essentials for upgrading ESXi

ESXi hosts can be upgraded from previous version or from ESXi 4.x in several ways. ESXi Installable 4.x hosts can be upgraded in one of three ways:

- An interactive upgrade via an ESXi Installable image
- A scripted upgrade, or using VUM. ESXi 5.0 hosts can be upgraded to 5.1
- The `esxcli` command-line tool

 If we have implemented Auto Deploy, we can directly apply a new image and reboot.

While upgrading VMware ESXi hosts from a previous version of ESXi 4.x to the latest version of 5.x using any of the three supported approaches, 50 MB must be accessible on the local VMFS volume. This space is required to store the ESXi server's configuration data in temp mode.

The following table illustrates approaches for upgrading ESXi to the latest version:

Upgrade approaches	From ESX/ESXi 4.x to ESXi 5.5	From ESXi 5.0 to ESXi 5.5	From ESXi 5.1 to ESXi 5.5
Using vSphere Update Manager	Possible	Possible	Possible
Using interactive upgrade from devices such as CD DVD or USB drive	Possible	Possible	Possible
Using scripted upgrade	Possible	Possible	Possible
Using vSphere Auto Deploy	Not Possible	Possible, **Key Note**: Only if the ESXi 5.0.x host was implemented using Auto Deploy	Possible, **Key Note**: Only if the ESXi 5.1.x host was implemented using Auto Deploy
Via `esxcli`	Not Possible	Possible	Possible

The following table illustrates the various scenarios that you will come across while upgrading ESXi to the latest version:

Scenario for Upgrade or Migration to ESXi 5.5	Support Status	How to do it
ESX and ESXi 3.x hosts	Direct upgrade is not possible	We must upgrade ESX/ESXi 3.x hosts to ESX/ESXi version 4.x before we can upgrade them to ESXi 5.5. Refer to the vSphere 4.x upgrade documentation. Alternatively, we might find it simpler and more cost-effective to perform a fresh installation of ESXi 5.5.
The ESX 4.x host that was upgraded from ESX 3.x with a partition layout incompatible with ESXi 5.x	Not possible	The VMFS partition cannot be preserved. Upgrading or migration is possible only if there is at most one VMFS partition on the disk that is being upgraded and the VMFS partition must start after sector 1843200. Perform a fresh installation. To keep virtual machines, migrate them to a different system.
ESX/ESXi 4.x host, migration or upgrade with vSphere Update Manager	Possible	Refer to the Using vSphere Update Manager to Perform Orchestrated Host Upgrades section in the vSphere Upgrade Guide.

Scenario for Upgrade or Migration to ESXi 5.5	Support Status	How to do it
ESX/ESXi 4.x host, interactive migration or upgrade	Possible	Refer to the Upgrade or Migrate Hosts Interactively section in the vSphere Upgrade Guide. The installer wizard offers the choice to upgrade or perform a fresh installation. If we upgrade, ESX partitions and configuration files are converted to be compatible with ESXi.
ESX/ESXi 4.x host, scripted upgrade	Possible	Refer to the Installing, Upgrading, or Migrating Hosts Using a Script section in the vSphere Upgrade Guide. In the `upgrade` script, specify the particular disk to upgrade on the system. If the system cannot be upgraded correctly because the partition table is incompatible, the installer displays a warning and does not proceed. In this case, perform a fresh installation. Upgrading or migration is possible only if there is at most one VMFS partition on the disk that is being upgraded and the VMFS partition must start after sector 1843200.
ESX 4.x host on a SAN or SSD	Partially possible	We can upgrade the host as we would normally upgrade a ESX 4.x host, but no provisions are made to optimize the partitions on the disk. To optimize the partition scheme on the host, perform a fresh installation.
ESX 4.x host, missing the Service Console .`vmdk` file, interactive migration from CD or DVD, scripted migration, or migration with vSphere Update Manager	Not possible	The most likely reasons for a missing Service Console are that the Service Console is corrupted or the VMFS volume is not available, which can occur if the VMFS was installed on a SAN and the LUN is not accessible. In this case, on the disk selection screen of the installer wizard, if we select a disk that has an existing ESX 4.x installation, the wizard prompts us to perform a clean installation.

Scenario for Upgrade or Migration to ESXi 5.5	Support Status	How to do it
ESX/ESXi 4.x host, asynchronously released driver or other third-party customizations, interactive migration from CD or DVD, scripted migration, or migration with vSphere Update Manager	Not possible	The most likely reasons for a missing Service Console are that the Service Console is corrupted or the VMFS volume is not available, which can occur if the VMFS was installed on a SAN and the LUN is not accessible. In this case, on the disk selection screen of the installer wizard, if we select a disk that has an existing ESX 4.x installation, the wizard prompts us to perform a clean installation.
ESX/ESXi 4.x host, asynchronously released driver or other third-party customizations, interactive migration from CD or DVD, scripted migration, or migration with vSphere Update Manager	Possible	When we upgrade an ESXi 5.0.x or 5.1.x host that has custom VIBs to Version 5.5, the custom VIBs are migrated. Refer to the Upgrading Hosts That Have Third-Party Custom VIBs section in the vSphere Upgrade Guide.
ESXi host 5.0.x	Possible	Methods supported for direct upgrade to ESXi 5.5 are: • vSphere Update Manager • Interactive upgrade from CD, DVD, or USB drive • Scripted Upgrade • `esxcli` • Auto Deploy If the ESXi 5.0.x host was deployed using Auto Deploy, we can use Auto Deploy to provide the host an ESXi 5.5 image.

Scenario for Upgrade or Migration to ESXi 5.5	Support Status	How to do it
ESXi 5.1.x host	Possible	Methods supported for direct upgrade to ESXi 5.5 are: • Sphere Update Manager. • Interactive upgrade from CD, DVD, or USB drive • Scripted Upgrade • esxcli • Auto Deploy If the ESXi 5.1.x host was deployed using Auto Deploy, we can use Auto Deploy to provide the host with an ESXi 5.5 image.

Design essentials for migrating ESXi

Migrating VMware ESXi 4.x to the latest version requires careful planning. The migration procedure will be affected by several factors—the version of VMware vCenter Server, the latest version of VMware ESXi, the compatibility of available hardware, boot considerations, and the type and destination state of data stores. We need a clear migration path. The outline of the migration plan is illustrated in the following section, and you can customize it according to your demands:

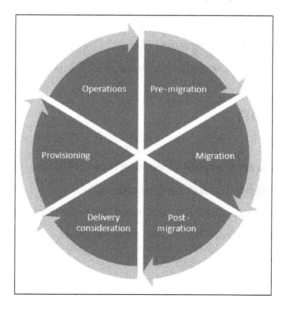

Pre-migration

The following pre-migration tasks should be performed prior to installing VMware ESXi on the host:

- Validate that all prerequisites are complete and verify that hardware requirements are met
- Document the existing VMware ESX host configuration
- Evacuate virtual machines and templates and put the host into Maintenance Mode
- If running in a VMware HA/VMware DRS cluster, remove the host from the cluster

Migration

After the pre-migration tasks are complete, you are ready to upgrade VMware ESXi and perform the migration.

The actual migration involves six steps:

- Removing the host from vCenter
- Installing VMware ESXi
- Configuring the management network
- Reconnecting the host in VMware vCenter Server
- Restoring host-specific configuration settings
- Testing/validating the upgraded host
- Moving the host back into the VMware HA/VMware DRS cluster

Post-migration

The following are generic considerations that are worth considering in your design:

- Configuring **Direct Console User Interface (DCUI)**
- Joining the ESXi host to **Active Directory (AD)**
- Identifying and configuring a persistent data store for configuring logging
- Backing up the VMware ESXi host configuration

Delivery considerations

Prior to redeployment of the ESX hosts to ESXi, you should run a testing phase that looks at the existing disposition and examines whether each element is suitable for ESXi. Obviously, a pilot is a good way to test the suitability of ESXi in your existing configuration. However, it's difficult to test every possible scenario via a small pilot. This is because large enterprises have many different types of hardware, versions of hardware, connections to different network and storage devices, backup tools, monitoring tools, and so on.

Provisioning

ESX servers can be upgraded or rebuilt. ESX 4.x server upgrades can be undertaken by the ESXi interactive or scripted install mechanism, or via VUM. If the ESX 4.x servers have previously been upgraded from ESX 3.x, then the partitioning configuration brought across might not allow a subsequent upgrade to ESXi. There needs to be at least 50 MB free in the host's local VMFS volume to store the previous configuration. If you're using VUM to upgrade, the /boot partition needs to have at least 350 MB free. If you don't have this much space, you can still use the interactive update because it doesn't need this space for staging the upgrade files. Any VMFS volumes on the local disk that need to be preserved must start after the first 1 GB; otherwise, the upgrade can't create the ESXi partitions it requires.

Operations

One of the more obvious techniques to smooth a transition is to begin using the newer cross-host management tools as early as possible. Most of the utilities available for ESX classic hosts work with ESXi hosts. vSphere Client, vCenter Server, vCenter Web Client, **vSphere command line interface** (**vCLI**), and PowerCLI are host-agnostic and will make any transition less disruptive. There is no reason not to start working with these tools from the outset; even if you decide not to migrate at that stage, you'll be better prepared when ESXi hosts begin to appear in your environment.

The primary management loss when you replace ESX is the Service Console. This is the one tool that, if you use it regularly, must be replaced with an equivalent. There are two main contenders: the vCLI and the ESXi Shell. The vCLI provides the same Linux-style commands as the Service Console. The easiest way to get it is to download the **vSphere Management Assistant** (**vMA**) virtual appliance. This includes a Linux shell and all the associated environmental tools you'd expect. Generally, anything you can do at a Service Console prompt, you can do in the vMA. Most scripts can be converted to vMA command syntax relatively easily. The second option is the ESXi Shell. Although it's a stripped-down, bare-bones environment, it provides the majority of vSphere-specific commands that you'd otherwise find in the Service Console. Some of the more Linux-centric commands may not be available, but it provides a more familiar feel than the vMA because it's host-specific, and therefore the syntax is closer to that of the Service Console.

In addition to rewriting scripts, you'll need to replace other services that ESX includes in the Service Console. For ESXi hosts without persistent storage for a scratch partition, it's important to either redirect the logs to a remote data store or configure the host to point to a remote syslog server. ESXi hosts don't have their own direct Web Access as ESX hosts do. It's unlikely that this is a regularly used feature but, if you've relied on it in certain circumstances, then you need to get accustomed to using the Windows client to connect to the host. Finally, if you've used the Service Console for host monitoring via SNMP or a server vendor's hardware agent, then ESXi has built-in CIM agents for hardware on the HCL. Many vendors can supply enhanced modules for their particular hardware. With these CIM modules; you can set up alerts in vCenter, and some third-party hardware-monitoring software can use the information. ESXi also provides some SNMP support, which you can use to replace any lost functionality of Service Console agents.

Designing essentials for the management layer

VMware vCenter Server provides a central platform for dealing with sVMware vSphere infrastructure. It is designed so as to automate and distribute a virtual infrastructure with assurance.

VMware vCenter is a key component in most centrally critical elements of our virtual data center. It's the management point we likely use to manage our virtual data center. We will create data centers, clusters, resource pools, networks, and data stores; assign permissions; configure alerts; and monitor performance. All of this functionality is centrally configured in the vCenter Server. You should therefore dedicate part of your design to building a robust and scalable vCenter Server, and the following diagram illustrates various components of vCenter from vSphere 5.1 and above:

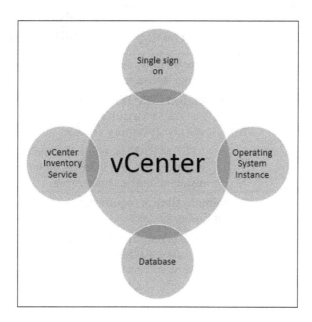

Before vSphere 5.1, vCenter Server was basically a monumental application; there were really only two major mechanisms to interact with: vCenter Server in vSphere 4.x and vSphere 5.0, which is an OS instance and **database**. However, with the introduction of vSphere 5.1, VMware has fragmented the monumental vCenter Server into a number of different components. In addition to the two previous components, **database** now joins another two components: **vCenter Inventory Service** and **Single Sign-On**.

The introduction of additional components in vSphere 5.1 and 5.5 means we also have to choose whether we will run all these components on a single server or break the roles apart on separate servers. Let's explore each component one by one.

OS instances and database requirements

VMware vCenter Server OS instances are available in two basic formats: installable software on the Windows platform or as a preinstalled virtual appliance that can work on Linux as part of the vCSA. Sizing vCenter Server Installable on a Windows platform must meet the following hardware requirements:

vCenter Server Hardware	Requirements
CPU	Two 64-bit CPUs or one 64-bit dual-core processor.
Processor	2.0 GHz or faster Intel 64 or AMD 64 processor.
Memory	Minimum memory requirements can be defined based on your design decision: • 4 GB of RAM is required if the vCenter Server is installed on a different server than vCenter SSO and vCenter Inventory Service • 10 GB of RAM is required if the vCenter Server, vCenter SSO, and vCenter Inventory Service are installed on the same server
Disk storage	Minimum storage requirements can be defined based on your design decision: • 4 GB is required if vCenter Server is installed on a different machine than vCenter SSO and vCenter Inventory Service • 40-60 GB is required if vCenter Server, vCenter SSO, and vCenter Inventory Service are installed on the same machine Disk storage requirements have to be calculated if the vCenter Server database runs on the same machine as vCenter Server. 450 MB is required for the log.
Microsoft SQL Server 2008 R2 Express disk	Up to 2 GB free disk space to decompress the installation archive. Approximately 1.5 GB is deleted after the installation is complete.
Network speed	Speed is 1 Gbps.

The vCenter Server Appliances are management applications that need sufficient resources in order to perform optimally. We should view the following as the minimum requirements for a specific to infrastructure. Oversizing vCenter Server might result in improved performance, better concurrency in production deployments, and reduced latency. Hardware requirements for VMware vCenter Server Appliances are as follows:

VMware vCenter Server Appliance Hardware	Requirements
Disk storage on the host machine	A minimum 70 GB and a maximum size of 125 GB are required. Disk space depends on the size of our vCenter Server inventory.
Memory in the VMware vCenter Server Appliance	If you are planning to use embedded PostgreSQL database, then vCenter Server appliance supports up to 100 ESXi hosts or 3,000 virtual machines and have the following memory requirements: • 8 GB is required for very small inventory (10 or fewer ESXi hosts, 100 or fewer virtual machines) • 16 GB is required for a small inventory (minimum of 10 to maximum of 50 ESXi hosts or minimum of 100 and maximum of 1,500 virtual machines) • 24 GB is required for a medium inventory (minimum of 50 to maximum of 100 ESXi hosts or minimum of 1,500 to maximum of 3,000 virtual machines) If you are planning to use an Oracle database, then vCenter Server appliance supports up to 1,000 ESXi hosts, 10,000 virtual machines, and 10,000 powered on virtual machines, and it has the following memory requirements: • 8 GB of ram required for a very small inventory (10 or fewer ESXi hosts, 100 or fewer virtual machines) • 16 GB of RAM required for small inventory (10 to 100 ESXi hosts or a minimum of 100 or maximum of 1,000 virtual machines) • 24 GB of RAM required for medium inventory (100 to 400 ESXi hosts or minimum of 1,000 or maximum of 4,000 virtual machines) • 32 GB of RAM required for a large inventory (more than 400 ESXi hosts or 4,000 virtual machines)

vCenter SSO

With the release of vSphere 5.1 and 5.5, VMware brought in a new feature to vCenter Server known as **vCenter Single Sign-On**. This component introduces a centralized verification facility that vCenter Server uses to allow for verification against multiple backend facilities, such as LDAP and AD.

For smaller environments, vCenter SSO can be installed on the same servers as the rest of the vCenter Server components; for larger environments, it can be installed on a different system for better performance. VMware vCenter SSO also supports a range of topologies, including standalone, cluster topology, and multisite topology.

The following table illustrates minimum hardware requirements for vCenter SSO, running on a separate host machine from vCenter Server:

vCenter SSO Hardware	Requirements
Processor	Intel or AMD x64 processor with a minimum two or more logical cores, each with a speed of 2 GHz
Memory	3 GB
Disk storage	2 GB
Network speed	1 Gbps

The components of SSO are **Security Token Service (STS)**, administration server, vCenter Lookup Service, and **VMware Directory Service**; these have to be considered while designing your infrastructure using SSO.

Deploying SSO models

VMware vCenter can be deployed using various methods such as Basic, Multiple SSO instances in the same location, and Multiple SSO instances in different locations.

Basic vCenter SSO

Basic vCenter SSO is the most well-known deployment mode and meets the requirements of most vSphere 5.1 and 5.5 users. Classically, this deployment model maintains the same methodology as previous vCenter Server infrastructure. In most cases, we can use **vCenter Simple Install** to deploy vCenter Server with vCenter SSO in the basic mode.

Multiple SSO instances in the same location

Using this deployment model, we install a vCenter SSO primary instance and one or more additional vCenter SSO instance on another node. Both the primary and secondary instances are sited behind a third-party network load balancer. Each vCenter SSO has its particular VMware Directory Service that replicates data with other vCenter SSO servers in the same location.

Multiple SSO instances in different locations

Using this deployment model, we can install different region-based deployments, when a single administrator needs to administer vCenter Server instances that are deployed on regionally dispersed sites in Linked Mode and each site is represented by one vCenter SSO, with one vCenter SSO on each HA cluster. The vCenter SSO site entry point is the system that other sites communicate with. This is the only system that needs to be accessible from the other sites. In a clustered deployment, the entry point of the site is the machine where the **HA load balancer** is installed.

vCenter Server Deployment	SSO Deployment Mode
Single vCenter Server	Basic vCenter SSO
Multiple local vCenter Servers	Basic vCenter SSO
Multiple remote vCenter Servers	Basic vCenter SSO
Multiple vCenter Servers in Linked Mode	Multisite vCenter SSO
vCenter Servers with high availability	Basic vCenter SSO with VMware vSphere HA (provides high availability for vCenter Server and vCenter SSO)
	Basic vCenter SSO with vCenter Server Heartbeat (provides high availability for vCenter Server and vCenter SSO)

VMware vCenter Inventory Service

In the next vCenter release, we can expect it to support cross **vCenter vMotion**. VMware also split off the inventory portion of vCenter Server into a separate component. The vCenter Inventory Service now provisions the discovery and management of inventory objects across different linked vCenter Server instances. As with vCenter SSO, we can install vCenter Inventory Service on the same system as the other components or we can split the Inventory Service onto a separate system for greater performance and scalability.

Design decisions for the management layer

In this section, we will discuss some of the key decisions involved in crafting the management layer design for your VMware vSphere infrastructure implementation, such as the following:

- Identifying vCenter to be hosted either on a physical server or on the VM Server

- Identifying vCenter to be hosted either on the Windows platform or VCA on the Linux platform

- Identifying database server locations either on primary sites or remote sites

- Configuration maximums to be considered

Let's get started straightaway with identifying decision-driving factors for installation and configuration.

Identifying whether vCenter will be hosted on a physical server or on VM Server

There is a long debate in the VMware blogs and community about whether we should install vCenter Server on a physical server or on VM. Let's take the case where we have a large enterprise that has some 200 ESXi hosts. For some reason, we have a serious outage. For example, we lose connectivity to LUN where vCenter VM is stored; we won't have the VM backup for another 6 to 12 hours. Consider that something goes wrong on our infrastructure. After VM boot, altogether we may have a high CPU and RAM usage. This is one example of what can happen if our vCenter is a virtual machine; another one could be in a **vCloud Director** (**vCD**) or **VMware Horizon infrastructure**; we cannot deploy any new VMs because our vCenter is down. We can't perform certain actions to restore our environment because we have no vCenter. As we can see, serious issues may arise if our virtual vCenter Server is not available.

We have discussed reasons for our infrastructure to have vCenter on physical hardware. Now, let's look at the other side of the coin: why we should choose to go for vCenter as a virtual machine. Note that VMware now lists the use of vCenter as a virtual machine as a best practice. Although it is best practice, there are certain risks and for those we have tabulated a migration plan as listed in the following table:

Failure reason	Design Justification
VMware vCenter is lost when the database fails	Design our SQL instances on a different server and cluster them
vCenter and SQL are VMs on the virtual infrastructure	Design vCenter and SQL on separate ESXis with anti-affinity rules set
vCenter and SQL belong to the same storage	Design our vCenter on different LUNs from storage devices
LUN connection failure to vCenter	Design database snapshots at periodic intervals
vCenter and SQL server has a performance challenge	Design our vCenter/SQL so it has adequate resources
VMware vCenter crashed	Deploy a new virtual machine to replace the crashed one and do not forget to attach it the database

Identifying whether vCenter will be hosted on the Windows platform or vCSA on the Linux platform

Identifying the correct vCenter is a key factor for your design. With vSphere 5.0 and 5.5, VMware introduced vCenter Server virtual appliance, which is a Linux-based virtual appliance. Prior to the introduction of the vCenter Server virtual appliance, we had only one option that is Windows platform-based: vCenter Server, let's see which option to pick for our design.

If we have a strong operational support for Microsoft Windows servers, which means a solid patching solution is in place, all critical alerts are monitored, and a proactive team of Windows administrators, it is best to deploy on a Microsoft Windows Server-based version of vCenter Server. This makes more sense than introducing a vCenter Server virtual appliance.

If you are looking for a simple and quick vCenter deployment and it is a smaller infrastructure, then go with a vCenter Server virtual appliance for very real benefits. Simply deploy the **Open Virtualization Format (OVF)** package, configure the vApp, and then hit the web-based management tool after that.

Identifying the database server location on primary sites or remote sites

Database manufacturers such as IBM, Microsoft, and Oracle recommend resource alignments for ideal performance of their database servers. For example, Microsoft recommends at least 1 GB of RAM and 4 GB for ideal performance of SQL Server.

On the other hand, take into consideration the resources required for the vCenter service, Web services, and plugins; we are looking at at least another 2 GB up to a maximum of 4 GB of RAM for vCenter. It is pretty likely that, in an enterprise infrastructure, our design has a properly sized database server that can accommodate the vCenter database without any major issues.

The recommended resources are as follows:

- 1 CPU with 2.0 GHz or any other similar configuration
- 4 GB of RAM

Taking this into account, if we install both the vCenter and the database server on the same server, we need at least 8 GB of RAM up to a maximum of 16 GB RAM and at least 4 CPUs up to a maximum of 8 CPUs. It is best to go for a local database for the preceding case. Based on your requirements, pick a local or remote database.

Configuration maximums to be considered

The maximum supported configurations that are required when you design your vSphere infrastructure are as follows:

vCenter Server Scalability	
Components	Configuration
ESXi hosts per vCenter Server	1,000
Powered-on VMs per vCenter Server	10,000
Registered VMs per vCenter Server	15,000
Linked vCenter Servers	10
ESXi hosts in linked vCenter Servers	3,000
Powered-on VMs in linked vCenter Servers	30,000
Registered VMs in linked vCenter Servers	50,000
Concurrent vSphere Client connections to vCenter Server	100
Concurrent vSphere Web Clients connections to vCenter Server	180
Number of ESXi hosts per datacenter	500

vCenter Server Scalability	
Components	Configuration
MAC addresses per vCenter Server	65,536
User Interface	
USB devices connected per vSphere Client	20
Concurrent operations	
vMotion operations per ESXi host (1 Gb/s network)	4
vMotion operations per ESXi host (10 Gb/s network)	8
vMotion operations per data store	128
Storage vMotion operations per ESXi host	2
Storage vMotion operations per ESXi data store	8
vCenter Server Appliance	
ESXi hosts (vPostgres database)	100
VMs (vPostgres database)	3,000
ESXi hosts (Oracle database)	1,000
VMs (Oracle database)	10,000
VMware vCenter Update Manager	
VMware Tools scan per ESXi host	90
VMware Tools upgrade per ESXi host	24
VM hardware scan per ESXi host	90
VM hardware upgrade per ESXi host	24
VMware Tools scan per VUM server	90
VMware Tools upgrade per VUM server	75
VM hardware scan per VUM server	90
VM hardware upgrade per VUM server	75
ESXi host scan per VUM server	75
ESXi host remediation per VUM server	71
ESXi host upgrade per VUM server	71
ESXi host upgrade per cluster	1
Cisco VDS update and deployment	70
VMware vCenter Orchestrator	
Associated vCenter Server systems	20
Associated ESXi instances	1,280
Associated VMs	350,001
Associated running workflows	300

Design considerations for management layers with industry inputs

Designing VMware vSphere is really challenging; to avoid any bottleneck, we need to learn and understand how it is really done by experienced architects in the following section. We will discuss the values and procedures that need to be followed while designing a VMware vSphere management layer, as we discussed in *Chapter 1, Essentials of VMware vSphere*.

Take into consideration the number of ESXi hosts and VMs we are going to have, followed by the kind of statistics we will need to maintain for our infrastructure. Sizing of server is most important from the ground up, so that we won't need to redeploy as we outgrow our infrastructure. Also, remember that our vCenter Server should be isolated from our database server, providing isolation of roles for the different components of the infrastructure. We should plan for resilience for both components and take into account what kind of outage we can predict. When we have this information, we can plan the level of resilience we need. Don't be afraid to design your vCenter as a VM. In some cases, this can deliver a greater level of resilience with more ease than using a physical server; hence, it is worth considering this option in your design.

vCenter is key to our kingdom of virtual infrastructure. Leaving it unprotected places your kingdom out in the open without security. A great number of attacks today are carried out from within the network.

It is always better to run infrastructure VMs on a dedicated virtual infrastructure (**cluster**), away from production. In each case, we will have to take into consideration what options are available to ensure that SLAs will not be violated. vCenter Server placement will also have an impact on the backup and recovery solution you will implement and on its licensing:

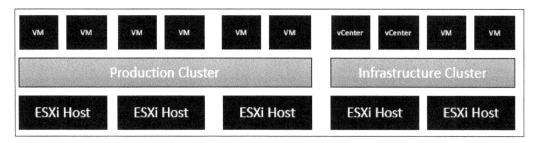

The following table lists the various design values and principles that every design is required to have:

Principles	Factors to consider
Readiness	Key components to consider on your design are as follows: • vSphere HA • DRS and Resource Pool • vCenter Heartbeat • Template and vMotion • Alarms and Statistics
Manageability	Key components to consider on your design are as follows: • Compatibility and interoperability • Scalability • Linked mode
Performance	Key components to consider on your design are as follows: • OS to be hosted • Database placement on either primary or secondary sites • Update Manager
Recoverability	Key components to consider on your design are as follows: • Recovery Time Objective (RTO) • Recovery Point Objective (RPO) • **Mean Time to Repair (MTTR)** • Disaster Recovery (DR) • Business Continuity (BC)
Security	Key components to consider on your design are as follows: • Isolation • SSL certificates • Domain certificates • Permission with right access and identity management
Justification	Key components to consider on your design are as follows: • Design decision • Risk and implications • Assumption and constraints

Finally, a monitoring utility needs to be installed in the guest OS. Make sure that your infrastructure monitoring utility will support the vCenter Server Appliances; otherwise, look for option monitoring via SSH or SNMP; vCenter Server Appliances have been improved in version 5.5. Enterprises must understand these considerations before selecting a vCenter Server Appliance as opposed to installing vCenter on Windows. Some further options are listed in the following table:

Features	vCenter on Windows platform	vCenter Server Appliances running on Linux platform
Linked Mode	Yes	No
Plugin	Yes	Partial
VMware HA	Yes	Yes
VMware FT	No	No
vCenter Heartbeat	Yes	No
VMware Update Manager	Yes	Partial
VMware SRM	Yes	Yes

Here are the various industry practices followed across different verticals and line of businesses:

- Key design principles should be followed while sizing a vCenter database appropriately to avoid performance issues.
- Never consider a built-in SQL Express database for production. It is configured to support only 5 ESXi hosts and no more than 50 virtual machines.
- Never disable DRS or use VM-Host affinity rules to decrease movements of vCenter.
- Using vSphere 5.5, we can implement SSO in a multisite configuration when vCenter Server Linked Mode is needed.
- Observe the effect of virtualizing vCenter. Ensure it has the highest priority for restarts and make sure that the services vCenter Server depends on are available – DNS, DHCP, AD, Database before that.
- If you are planning to use SRM for DR, it is recommended to consider using separate Windows instances for installation of SRM including **Storage Replication Adapters** (**SRAs**).
- If you're planning to install vCenter Server along with other VMs, set CPU and memory shares to the maximum.

- In large enterprise virtual infrastructures, make VMware vCenter as isolated as possible by scaling out rather than having all roles such as Inventory, SSO, VUM, and SRM on the same Windows instance.

- Perform proper sizing of vCenter resource while adding any other management components, such as vCOPS, SRM, and VUM.

- Implement vCenter as a VM or vCSA to make use of its advantages over virtualization. This will help you achieve server consolidation.

- Justify RTO, RPO, and MTTR for vCenter in your design document.

- Optimize multiple idle sessions within vCenter if the Windows terminal server is not set to the ideal timeout.

- Sizing vCenter should have considerations for further scalability, including clusters and VM accommodation.

- Design essentials should provide necessary information such as whether VM should have clocks synchronized. This will avoid unpredictable results during the installation and configuration of SSO.

- Design should advise the deployment of vCenter Server to configure the Managed IP address.

- Back up vCenter Server on a periodic basis and test the recovery procedure periodically. This should act as a health check on your design document.

Summary

In this chapter, you read about the design essentials for ESXi, design of ESXi, design configurations of ESXi, design considerations for ESXi with industry inputs, design essentials for upgrading ESXi, design essentials for migrating ESXi, designing essentials for management layer, design decisions for the management layer, and design considerations for management layer with industry inputs. In the next chapter, you will learn about designing VMware vSphere Networking.

3
Designing VMware vSphere Networking

VMware vSphere is a promising virtualization product. Though we may have the desire to begin deployment straightaway, heed the motto of the VMware vSphere network design before you start. We must look at several prerequisites even before we install the VMware vSphere product on our VT-enabled hardware; failing to meet any one of these prerequisites could entail a lot of troubleshooting. Also, another complexity during unplanned deployment is that you will end up with a greater risk of outage on other servers and systems as well. Communication with shared storage, and networks without the requisite preparation may involuntarily take down other servers and systems or in the worst case, this action could cause irretrievable data loss. If you are planning to operate with VMware ESXi in the very first attempt, take the required amount of time. Pay attention to the planning phase; in return, this will save time in the long run. Reading this book will not only ensure that you avoid hours of troubleshooting, but it will also cover core knowledge gained from best practices, derived from numerous lessons learned from previous deployments across different industries. In this chapter, you will learn the essentials of vSphere networking, getting started with vSphere, setting the properties of vSphere, and so on.

This chapter provides an overview of your vSphere networking and design essentials. Looking at our system from a high level, we can see where vSphere network virtualization best fits into the environment. Before you begin with your mission, let's quickly explore the basic definitions that are used in networking circles; they are seen in the following table:

Term	Description
Switch	This is a hardware networking device that aids as a controller and enables devices, such as computers, printers, servers, and so on, to communicate with each other.

Term	Description
Router	This is a hardware networking device that helps to direct (route, which is the reason for the name) data/information from one network (LAN) to another (LAN).
Bridge	This networking device helps to connect to two or more different networks. It is similar to a router, but it analyzes whether the data is being forwarded.
NIC	This stands for **Network Interface Controller** (**NIC**). It is a networking device that helps to connect one system to another over the network.
NIC Teaming	A collection of multiple uplink adapters are connected to each other to form a team in a single switch. A team can either section the burden of traffic between the virtual networks and physical network or deal passive failovers in the event of a network outage, hardware failure, power failure, or DC outage.
VPN	This stands for **Virtual Private Network** (**VPN**), a private communication network that is usually used within a private company to communicate from a public network.
Packet switching	This swaps data throughout the Internet. Most data is reduced to smaller packets before the transfer and then reunited at the destination.
VLAN	This stands for Virtual Local Area Network. It is a broadcast domain created by a switch.
Physical network	This network enables physical machines with their regions to communicate with each other. It also enables the flow of data. VMware ESXi runs on a physical machine.
Physical Ethernet switch	Physical adapter or uplink controls the network traffic across systems over the physical network. A switch contains several ports, each of which can be associated with its own physical system or another switch over the network.
Virtual network	On this network, VMs running on a host are interconnected sensibly to each other in order to send and receive data from other VMs.
Virtual adapter	This is a network that enables VMs to communicate with each other. Based on this connection, communication in terms of data flows between VMs and physical machines.

In this chapter, we will cover the following topics:

- VMware vSphere networking essentials
- Designing **VMware vSphere Standard** (**VSS**) and **VMware Distributed Switches** (**VDS**)
- Determining factors that influence the virtual network
- Designing the VMware vSphere network
- Design considerations for networking layers with industry inputs

VMware vSphere networking essentials

VMware vSphere is the largest and most powerful server virtualization suite used across the globe. It is a stepping stone to software-defined datacenters that use the VMware vCD or your own defined cloud-based datacenter. The VMware vSphere suite provides the flexibility and reliability to compute resources by merging available resources and converting them into an aggregated pool of resources. It has a proven record of high availability, scalability (on demand), fault tolerance, and security. The VMware vSphere suite seamlessly provides **vCompute**, **vStorage**, and the **vNetwork** virtualization layer for aggregated physical resources to operate across datacenters. The following diagram illustrates this flexibility across datacenters:

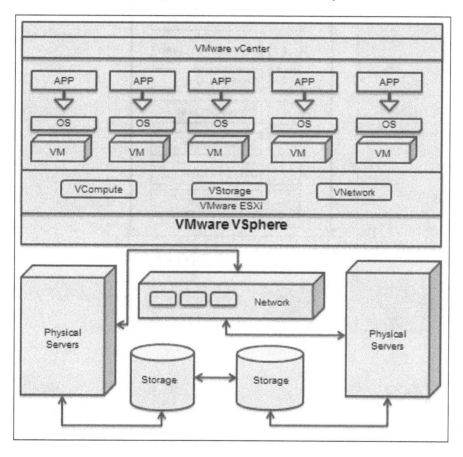

The VMware vSphere virtual switch works in a manner similar to the network layer 2 physical switch. Before we begin with the virtual switch network, let's first look at the networking **Open Systems Interconnection** (**OSI**) model, which is the very basic model of the networking world. A computer network is a collection of two or more systems linked together with the main objective of data or information sharing. ISO, along with the IEC-defined standard model for networking, which is called OSI, consists of seven layers as illustrated here:

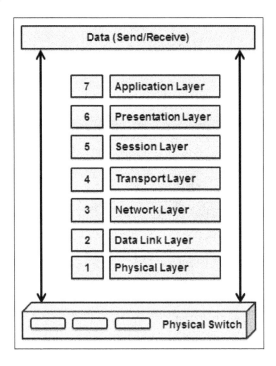

Now, let's explore how to connect the network with VMware vSphere. The vSphere virtual switch is a software layer that allows VMs to communicate with one another. This virtual switch can communicate intelligently with data flows on the network by examining data packets before sending them. The complete communication flow is illustrated here:

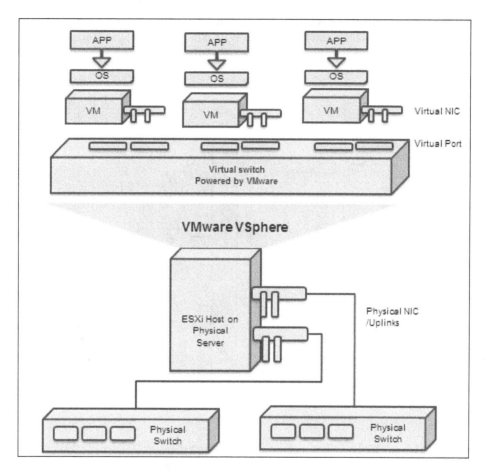

The design of VMware VSS and VDS

The VMware vSphere virtual switch is classified into two features, VMware VSS and VMware VDS.

Using the VMware VSS is like using a physical switch; each VMware vSphere ESXi host has its personal virtual switches. It automatically detects where the VM is connected and forwards the packet accordingly. The vSphere Distributed Switch is one virtual switch that is shared across multiple ESXi hosts and acts as a single switch across the associated ESXi host:

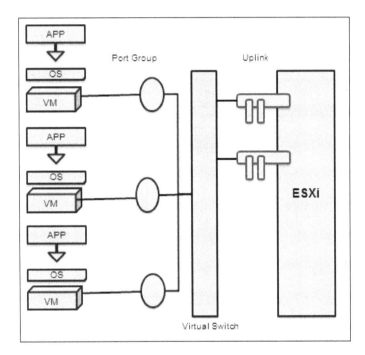

On the virtual switch, the left-hand side shows **port groups** linked to it; they are connected to VMs. On the left-hand side are **uplink** connecters that are linked to physical Ethernet adapters on the associated ESXi host. A VM communicates with the physical environment via physical Ethernet adapters that are plugged into the virtual switch adapter. Virtual switches in ESXi are built and operated in the VMkernel. Virtual switches are also called vSwitches.

 We cannot telnet in a vSwitch. There is no command-line interface for a vSwitch, apart from the VMware vSphere CLI. Here is an example:

```
vicfg-vswitch
```

In spite of these similarities, VMware switches have more variations compared to physical switches. The VMware vSwitch does not use dynamic negotiations for the creation of 802.1q trunks, **Port Aggregation Protocol (PAgP)**, or port channels such as **Dynamic Trunking Protocol (DTP)**. In any case, vSwitch cannot be linked to another vSwitch, thus eradicating a possible loop configuration. vSwitches do not run **Spanning Tree Protocol (STP)** since looping is a well-known network problem.

Now, let's go ahead and talk about vSphere switches. There are a few things that you need to know: VSSes are created per host. They are unique for each host because they are created on each one. The name of the port group should be unique because this will be validated for the purpose of working with vMotion:

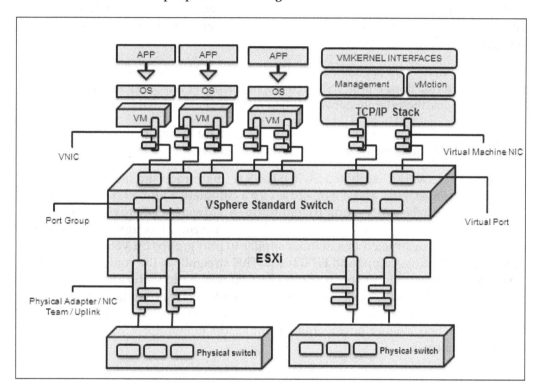

The standard switch is generally used to establish a communication between the physical host (ESXi) and VMs. A VSS can fulfill the gap of circulation internally between the VMs in the identical VLAN, and it aids communication with external networks as well.

In order to set up communication between the physical host (ESXi) and the VM running on the same ESXi, we have to connect a physical NIC in the ESXi to the physical uplink ports on the VSS. VMs have virtual NICs that we connect to port groups on the same standard switch. Wherever the uplinks are connected to each port group, they can utilize one or more physical NICs to allow VM network traffic and network load balancing. If we are already notice that on the vSphere Client console a port group does not have a physical NIC associated to it, the VM on the identical port group can connect with the other VM within the ESXi, but not outside its reach.

A VSS models an Ethernet switch. By default, the number of logical ports for VSS is 120. We are allowed to attach one NIC of a VM to each of its port. Each uplink adapter linked with a VSS utilizes one port. Every logical port on the VSS is a single port group of some sort.

While two or more VMs are associated with the identical VSS, any network circulation between them functions within ESXi. If a physical adapter is associated with the VSS, each VM can use the external network when it is associated with the adapter.

VSS port groups are groups of numerous ports that are in a mutual configuration with each other and bring a stable point for the VM that joins considered networks.

A VMware vNetwork Distributed Switch has a configuration similar to vSwitch from the ESXi host level, and it helps to set up a cumulative unified datacenter level. VMware VDS can be easily administered through VMware vSphere clients who are mandatorily committed to the vCenter Server. As vSwitch comprises VDS port groups that are constructed in a manner similar to port groups on VSS, VDS port groups extend across compound ESXi hosts. This streamlines the configuration of VMs across compound ESXi hosts and enables an easy build that VMware vMotion is capable of. VDS port groups maintain the network port state centrally as VMs, either for planned or unplanned migration from one ESXi host to another using VMware vMotion. This empowers reliable indicators to monitor VMs against exposure to intrusion.

The following diagram illustrates the high-level configuration of the VDS. The VMware VDS abstracts the configuration of vSwitch from the host level to a collective centralized datacenter level. The VMware vNetwork Distributed Switch is managed through VMware vSphere clients that are committed to VMware vCenter Server:

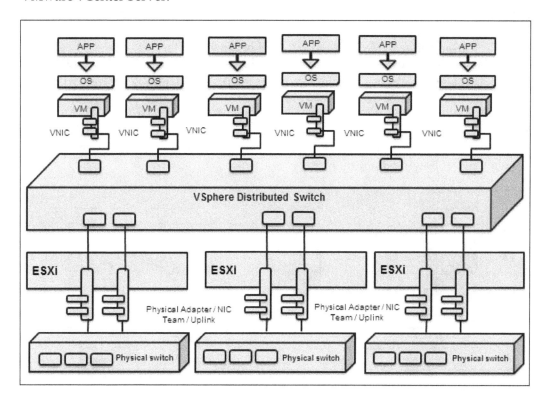

This section will explain not only the architecture of vSphere Distributed Switch, but also its core components, networking configurations, along with the management of ESXi hosts that are connected to the switch that is centralized on the vCenter system. Every host is connected to a host proxy switch that contains the networking settings for the ESXi host that are configured on VMware vSphere Distributed Switch. The VMware VDS contains a minimum of one or a maximum of 5000 VDS port groups. The main reason behind using VDS port groups is to fulfill networking communication between VMs and also to make space for the VMkernel traffic. We have to assess this in order to find each and every VDS port group via its network name (also called a network label). During the process of assigning a name, we must ensure that we provide a unique network label or network name. A record of every VDS port group that we create via the vCenter server is created on each ESXi host that is related to VDS. We need to create a rule for a VDS port group; this rule will be consistent for all hosts in the Distributed Switch. Now, let's explore the architecture shown in the following diagram:

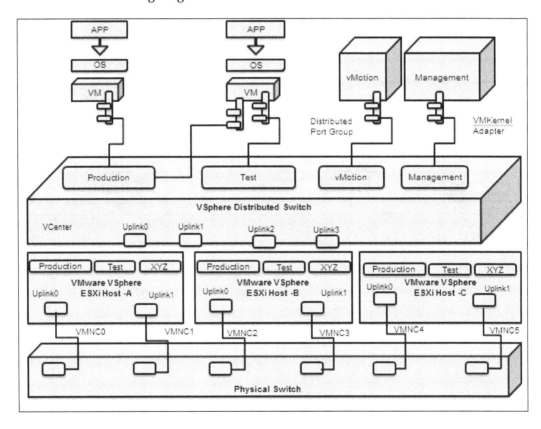

From a functional standpoint, VDS offers a unified control through which we can install, configure, monitor, and administer VM networks for our enterprise datacenter. Apart from these, the other major functionalities are as follows:

- Straightforward alignment of VM networks
- Boosted network monitoring and troubleshooting
- Modern, advanced networking features

Let's explore the listed benefits one by one in the upcoming sections. In VDS, the straightforward alignment of VM networks aids the following choices:

- The VMware VDS key aligns the administration, provisioning, configuration, management, and monitoring of virtual networks across each ESXi host on the datacenter
- The VMware vSphere's distributed switch assists an administrator with control over the following:
    - VDS port group naming
    - VDS port configurations
    - VDS screen settings
    - **Link Aggregation Control Protocol (LACP)**

What is LACP?

LACP is a component that aids transfers and automatically arranges link aggregation among vSphere hosts and the physical switch access layer.

On VDS, there are boosted network monitoring and troubleshooting functionalities. The VMware VDS is key in aligning administration with respect to monitoring and troubleshooting proficiencies. VDS aids the administrator with the monitoring and troubleshooting of the following features:

- RSPAN, ERSPAN, SNMP v3, and IPFIX NetFlow v10
- A network health check is performed to validate whether vSphere has compunction with physical network configurations
- Troubleshooting rollbacks, updates, and recoveries over various phases of administration

- Troubleshooting backup and restore operations on VMs with template configurations over various phases of administration

- Troubleshooting netdumps (network-based core dumps used to debug hosts without even the need for local storage) over various phases of administration

Here are the advanced networking features that aid the following choices:

- VDS offers support for advanced networking features, such as traffic management and bidirectional VM rate limiting, along with modern and advanced networking-management features. These features are listed as follows:

  ○ VDS offers administrator support for core components, such as NetIOC, SR-IOV, and BPBU screening, which are explained here:

> What is NetIOC?
>
> VMware vSphere VDS **Network Input Output Control** (NetIOC) is used to configure instructions and guidelines at the VM level and ensure that the input and output resources are continuously offered for our business-critical applications. NetIOC monitors the network. Whenever it sees jamming or blocking, it spontaneously shifts assets to our highest-priority applications, as demarcated by our business rules.
>
> What is SR-IOV?
>
> VMware vSphere VDS **Single Root I/O Virtualization** (**SR-IOV**) is an arrangement that allows a PCIe (PCI Express is a high-speed serial bus that functions more like a network compared to bus) device to appear to be many separate physical PCIe devices.
>
> What is BPBU?
>
> VMware vSphere VDS **Bridge Protocol Data Units** (**BPDU**) data contains frame information regarding the switch ID, starting switch port, switch port priority, MAC address, and switch port cost.

  ○ VDS offers administrator support for third-party vSwitch lean-tos, such as IBM 5000V and Cisco Nexus 1000V

Let's now go ahead and explore the terminology used in VDS. A detailed classification of these is given in the following table:

Terms	Description
DV port groups (VDS virtual port groups)	They specify the port configuration choices for every member port within the virtual switch
Distributed Virtual Uplinks (dvUplinks)	They provide a smooth layer for physical NICs on every ESXi host across datacenters
Private Virtual Local Area Networks (PVLANs)	They aid wider compatibility with the available networking infrastructure
Network vMotion	This streamlines the checking and fixing of problems by tracking the networking status of each and every VM as it moves from one ESXi host to another on a VDS
Bidirectional traffic shaping	This applies the traffic-shaping rule on the VDS port group and is defined by the average bandwidth, burst size, and peak bandwidth
Third-party virtual switch support	This offers a stretch for the integration of third-party data planes, control planes, and user interfaces, with the IBM 5000V and Cisco Nexus 1000V

We will discuss the key enhancements you can find in VMware VSphere 5.5 now. Network health can be monitored, and a report on it can be viewed. The VDS configuration can be backed up and restored on demand. The management network recovery option can be used in the event of a failure. The rollback option has been provided for maintenance periods. Additionally, scalability enhancements have been made. Apart from these, features, such as LCAP, BPDU, and SR-IOV (as you learned in the previous section) are also considered as key additions in VMware VSphere 5.5.

Now, let's go ahead and look at a comparison between VSS and VDS. The following table compares the features of VMware VDS against those of VMware VSS. While VSS is available by default in all editions of VMware vSphere, VDS is only available in the VMware vSphere Enterprise Plus edition. Moreover, VMware vCenter is mandatory for VDS administration; however, this is not the case for VSS. We can manage VSS via the vSphere Client. The following table compares the features of VSS and VDS:

Features	VSS	VDS
Switching features		
Support for Layer 2 Forwarding	Available	Available
Support for IEEE 802.1Q VLAN tagging	Available	Available
Support for Multicast support	Available	Available
Support for vMotion Network Policy	NA	Available
Physical switch features		
Support for EtherChannel	Available	Available
Support for load-balancing algorithms on the virtual port ID	Available	Available
Support for source Mac	Available	Available
Support for source and destination IP	Available	Available
Operational features		
Support for Tx rate limiting (network traffic management feature)	Available	Available
Support for Rx rate limiting (network traffic management feature)	NA	Available
Support for port security (security feature)	Available	Available
Support for VMSafe compatibility (security feature)	Available	Available
Support for Private VLANs (security feature)	NA	Available
Support for VMware vCenter support (management feature)	Available	Available
Support for third-party accessible APIs (management feature)	Available	Available
Support for network policy groups (management feature)	Available	Available
Support for NetFlow v5 (management feature)	Available	Available
Support for CDP v1/v2 (management feature)	Available	Available

Determining factors that influence virtual networks

Virtualization enables the collective use of hardware resources. Hence, it is an important factor, specifically for server consolidation when it comes to saving management, space, and energy costs. One research area is the network. It is definitely difficult to identify factors that will create a performance bottleneck; hence, we will start with the following influencing factors:

- Choosing a physical switch
- Choosing the right virtual switch
- Sizing the Ethernet capacity
- Choosing the right enhancers
- Choosing the ESXi server architecture to accommodate the network

The listed factors are crucial. You may consider other factors based on your requirements; hence, this is not a comprehensive list of factors, but this is more than enough to get started.

Choosing a physical switch

Let's get started with the physical switch. Your switch should have features, capabilities, and protocols to support your design. Features should play an important role in decisions regarding your vSphere network design. Some of the more considerable parts of chains that we should take into account or identify as factors are as follows:

- Link aggregation control protocol
- Private VLANs
- TSO and jumbo frames

Keep in mind that your physical switch's support for additional technologies is enough to vastly influence your virtual datacenter.

LACP enthusiastically negotiates link aggregation parameters, such as the number of Uplinks across VDS, hashing algorithms, and physical access layer switches. If link outage or cabling mistakes occur, the LACP repeatedly renegotiates parameters across the two switches. This reduces the manual interference needed to debug cabling issues. It has improved a lot in vSphere 5.5 and has the following enchantments:

- Comprehensive load-balancing algorithm supports 22 new hashing algorithm options
- Comprehensive multiple link aggregation groups support 64 LAGs per ESXi host, and 64 LAGs per VDS are supported
- LACP can be provisioned via the VMware vSphere template

Managed datacenter switches are enabled with link aggregation support, so we might speculate as to why link aggregation has its own section to act around. Well, there are specific key deliberations around LACP that we need to talk about in our design. For our case, we might need to question ourselves about the capabilities of the LACP in our physical switches. Here are some of these questions:

- How do we identify that the physical switch is capable to supporting link-aggregation?
- How do we identify the type of link that has the capability of supporting aggregation of the switch?
- How do we identify that a multiswitch link aggregation can support a switch?
- How do we identify that load-balancing approaches are supported to route traffic on the connections in the aggregate approach?

The answer to these questions can have an influence on our vSphere network design and can also encourage accurate designs.

PVLAN permits users to rationally subdivide physical network segments into dispersed broadcast domains. VLANs are classically linked with an IP subnets so that every VLAN is comparable to an IP subnet. For systems in dissimilar VLANs to interconnect, they should pass their traffic via a router. The design of VLAN for vSphere environments should be planned based on requirements. So, the following are essential to a better understanding of VLANs:

- A comprehensive variety of physical switches should be openly configured to provide a link to a VLAN trunk. In case we are not configuring the links associated to our ESXi hosts as VLAN trunks, then VLAN will not work on our virtual infrastructure.

- A wide variety of VLAN deployments provides a lone VLAN that doesn't convey any VLAN tags. Based on the vendor, this VLAN strength be stated as an untagged VLAN or native VLAN.

- Reliably allocate untagged or native VLANs across each switch port to get a command for connectivity output.

- Make sure that your physical switches have the capability to support end-to-end virtualization requirements; if not, the design should be customized according to this specification.

Private VLANs are associated with normal VLANs, but there are high-class benefits over normal VLANs. For case, VLANs are characteristically connected to an IP subnet, and there is no informal way to edge communications in a particular VLAN or a related subnet. On the other hand, PVLAN authorized users to control communiqué among VMs on the same VLAN or network section; which become a vital influence in your network virtualization design.

Now, let's explore the different types of Private VLAN to help with design essentials. Private VLAN is separated into two kinds: primary VLAN and secondary VLAN. Secondary VLAN is further classified into three kinds, such as promiscuous, isolated, and community types, as shown in the following diagram.

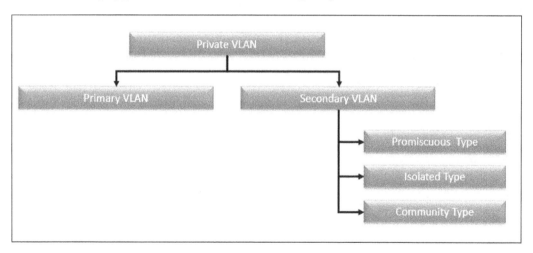

The following table illustrates the various definitions of PVLANs:

Classification	Description
Primary PVLAN	The unique VLANs that have been alienated into smaller groups are said to be primary PVLAN.
Secondary PVLAN	PVLAN has a precise VLAN ID related to it. Each packet interconnects via its labelled data packet with a VLAN ID as if it were a usual VLAN.
Promiscuous	PVLANs can interconnect via the router to additional devices in other VLANs. A node devoted to a port in an immoral secondary PVLAN could send and receive packets to any other node in any other secondary PVLAN linked to the identical primary PVLAN.
Isolated	The isolated type will not interconnect to any other ports in the same inaccessible secondary PVLAN or from a community PVLAN. A node devoted to a port in an inaccessible secondary PVLAN could transfer packets from a promiscuous PVLAN.
Community	The community kind will neither interconnect to nodes in other community secondary PVLANs nor interconnect to nodes in an inaccessible secondary PVLAN.

The following diagram illustrates the communication mechanism between each of PVLAN types specific to the secondary PVLAN:

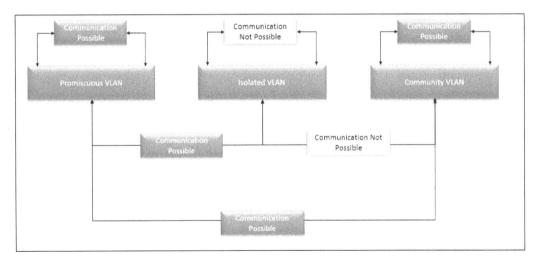

In your design, if you want to use PVLANs, you need a physical switch that can support PVLANS. Not all physical switches support PVLANs. Make sure that you identify the switch support while you choose the switches for your vSphere design.

The objective of using **TCP Segmentation Offload (TSO)** in VM and VMkernel NICs is to improve the performance of the network and reduce the CPU overhead for TCP operations over networks so that the host CPU can be used for many applications.

TSO resides on the path of physical transmission and VM NIC. This helps to improve the ESXi performance. Whenever TSO is enabled, the NIC divides larger data masses into TCP segments in place of the CPU. The host can use more CPU cycles to run applications.

We can allow TSO support on a VM via a boosted VMXNET adapter; in order to allow TSO in the Virtual Machine, it is necessary to alter the present VMXNET or elastic virtual NIC with improved VMXNET. This will help to make sure that the alteration has taken place in the MAC address. Also, certain prerequisites are available to enable TSO. For example, the VM should have one of the following OS

- Red Hat Enterprise Linux 4 specific to 64-bit
- Red Hat Enterprise Linux 5 specific to both 32-bit and 64-bit
- SUSE Linux Enterprise Server 10 specific to both 32-bit and 64-bit
- Microsoft Windows Server 2003 Enterprise Edition with Service Pack 2 specific to both 32-bit and 64-bit

Choosing the right virtual switch

After designing the physical network layer, the next step is to design the access layer where the VM will interact with the physical switch. In this chapter, you have learned enough about the design of VSS and VDS earlier. By now, you should have a broader understanding of the benefits and usability of both virtual switches; each kind of virtual switch has its own set of merits and demerits.

Let's get started by comparing VSS to VDS. Some of the following features are available on both kinds of virtual switches:

- Capacity to move L2 frames from one stage to another stage
- Capacity to perform section traffic in VLANs
- Capacity to utilize and accommodate the 802.1q VLAN encapsulation
- Capacity to put up one Uplink, which involves nothing but teaming with NIC
- Capacity to handle traffic shaping for the TX egress's outbound traffic

On the other hand, the following features are only available in VDS. Hence, you should preferably pick a virtual switch that will preferably go with VDS:

- Inbuilt capacity to shape inbound (RX ingress) traffic
- Inbuilt capacity to use insistent network VMotion
- Inbuilt capacity to centrally manage VDS via vCenter
- Inbuilt capacity to support PVLANs and LACP for dynamic link aggregation configuration
- Inbuilt capacity to handle load-based NIC teaming
- Inbuilt ability to import/export VDS configurations

Ethernet capacity sizing

Modern datacenters and enterprises believe that 10 GB has more benefits than 1 GB. Some of the facts that follow on from this are:

- It is always recommended that you use two 10 GB for HA, which will provide greater redundancy over 10 or more 1 GB Ethernets
- Using 10 GB Ethernet decreases the quantity of ports demanded when likened to 1 GB Ethernet
- 10 GB requires fewer ports; wires between systems will be reduced

Although 10 GB Ethernet can deal out welfare to a VMware vSphere infrastructure, several considerations should be taken into account while designing infrastructure with 10 GB Ethernet; these are tabulated in the following table:

Components	Essentials
Datacenter physical network cable	Design essentials should consider the limitations of network design, and correct recommendations, such as Cat-6A cabling should be considered as a mitigation.
Datacenter physical switches	Most vendors offer 10 GB Ethernet-based capable switches. When we design our virtual datacenter, we should take into consideration our current and future demands as well.

Components	Essentials
Ethernet network partitioning in hardware	Let's assume that you opted to go for 10 GB Ethernet; on your design, don't allot 10 GB Ethernet for IP storage or vMotion. As we discussed earlier, some vendors offer the capability for the classification of a single 10 GB Ethernet link in hardware, so we can classify the classes as follows: • 3 GB for IP storage • 3 GB for VM traffic • 2 GB for FT • 1 GB for a management port • 1 GB for vMotion

A majority of vSphere designers include 10 GB Ethernet in their designs, this provides an alternate solution to inflexibilities offered by multiple 1 GB Ethernet NICs; potentially, though, another way to remove those rigidities is to use a new technology called **I/O virtualization**.

Choosing the right enhancers

In vSphere's latest version, a lot of network enhancements, such as the following ones, are made by providing more flexibility to systems:

• Network I/O Control

• NetQueue

• SR-IOV

• DirectPath I/O

Let's get started with the VMware vSphere Network I/O Control. This provides support while partitioning the network capacity during contention. Network I/O Control delivers add-on control over the utilization of bandwidth in the form of network limits and isolation. VMware vMotion processes provisional network traffic that tries to eat as much bandwidth as possible.

VMware vSphere Network Resource Pools regulate the bandwidth against VDS. On every VMware vSphere network, the input/output control option is set to be enabled.

The VDS traffic is divided into the components of VMware vSphere Network Resource Pools, as follows:

- Management
- Fault tolerance
- NFS
- vSphere replication
- vMotion
- VM
- iSCSI

VMware vSphere offers the preceding components as user-specified:

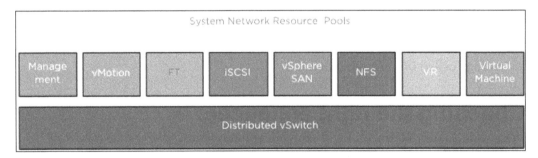

We are also allowed to form network resource pools to control VM traffic through the bandwidth by configuring its physical NIC dividends and host boundary. The following diagram illustrates the Network I/O logical design:

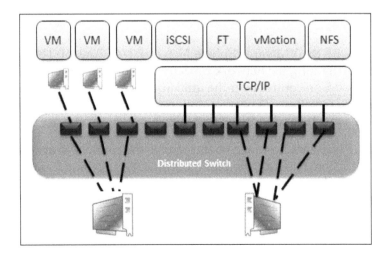

In a nutshell, VMware vSphere Network I/O Control helps to configure rules and policies at the VM level and ensures that Input Output resources are continuously obtainable for our mission-critical applications. Network I/O Control monitors the network. When it sees mobbing, it robotically diverts resources to our highest-priority applications.

NetIOC arms administrators with the following capabilities:

Type	Description
Isolation	This aids traffic isolation so that a provided flow will never govern others and foil drops.
Shares	This helps to allow elastic networking bulk partitioning to deal with overcommitment when flows compete for same resources.
Limits	This limits the administrative traffic bandwidth frontier on the whole VDS set of dvUplinks.
Load-based teaming	This uses a VDS set of dvUplinks for networking volume.
IEEE 802.1p tagging	These tag outbound packs from the vSphere ESXi host for proper treatment by physical network capitals.

Thanks to NetIOC, our administrators can be more productive. We can extend virtualization across more workloads, and our virtual infrastructure can become more versatile.

Let's look at the enhancer that is available. VMware vSphere NetQueue offers the benefit of the volume of network adapters to carry network traffic to the ESX/ESXi host in many received queues that can be managed distinctly, thus permitting them to be mounted to numerous CPUs and refining the networking performance of the receive-side.

The kernel feature of VMware vSphere is NetQueue, which offloads packet routing to VMs on the VMware ESX host, thus releasing CPU resources and reducing latency. NetQueue permits all the virtual network adapters to have a network queue in place of one common queue.

From ESX 4.0 onwards, by default, VMware hosts are enabled on all NetQueue.

The following syntax helps to check whether the configuration is accurate:

```
#esxcfg-module -g bnx2x#esxcfg-module-gs2io (for the Neterion)
#esxcfg-module-g ixgbe (for the Intel)
```

Next, remember that there is no strategic technique defined from VMware to test this. **NetI/O meter** and **IxChariot** are two third-party tools that will aid in tracing networks and can give a defined output of bandwidth and net load on RX/TX queues.

NetQueue is required to be configured on ESXi at three different levels:

- From the ESXi OS level, enabled by default
- From the driver level
- From the hardware layer

A third enhancer is available. VMware vSphere DirectPath I/O is an efficient technology that is accessible from the latest version of VMware. It controls hardware chains, such as Intel VT-d and AMD-Vi, and in turn, allows guests to directly access hardware schemes. VMware DirectPath I/O will not support many structures, such as memory overcommit, vMotion, physical NIC sharing, and NetIOC. As a result of this, it is recommended that you use DirectPath I/O only for heavy jobs with very huge packet rates.

Enabling passthrough devices provides the means to use resources efficiently and improve the performance of your environment. You can enable the DirectPath I/O passthrough for a network device on a host.

VMware vSphere VMDirectPath gives the guest OS direct access on an I/O device, avoiding the virtualization level. This passthrough, by pass, or direct path can provide a huge growth recital for a VMware ESXi host by applying a high-speed I/O policy on the devices:

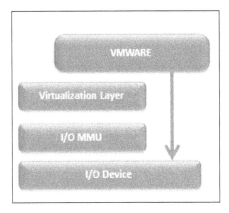

VMware vSphere VMDirectPath I/O can assist a guest OS whenever there is a need for a better recital from the ESXi host I/O device.

The difficulty of utilizing VMware VMDirectPath I/O is that a majority of the features will be unavailable, such as VMotion, record and replay, suspend and resume, fault tolerances, hot add and remove of virtual devices, DRS, HA, and snapshots. However, if we are using VMDirectPath 1/O on a CISCO UCS VM-FEX distributed system, it will allow us to have the features mentioned earlier.

A fourth enhancer is also available. VMware vSphere 5.1 and future releases provision Single Root I/O virtualization. We can use SR-IOV to interact with VMs that are inactivity-sensitive or require extra CPU resources.

Single root I/O virtualization is a description that permits only a Peripheral Component Connect Express on a physical device below a single root port to seem as multiple discrete physical devices to the host or VM:

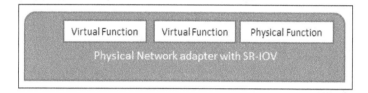

Single Root I/O virtualization utilizes the physical functions and virtual functions to accomplish global functions for SR-IOV devices. Physical functions are full PCI utilities that are proficient in arranging and running the SR-IOV functionality. It is designed to organize or switch PCIe devices using physical functions, and the physical functions have the full capacity to change data flows in and out of the systems. VFs are lightweight PCI, meaning that they support data flows, but have a limited set of configuration incomes.

The number of virtual functions delivered to the host or VM will be contingent on the device. PCIe devices enabled by SR-IOV involve good BIOS and hardware chains as well as SR-IOV chains in the VM driver or host instance.

Adapting the ESXi server architecture to accommodate the network

The architecture of ESXi servers can have a great impact on our vSphere network design in different ways. A few of the comprehensible effects on your network design include the following (it is worth considering these components on your server specifications):

- The ESXi server design controls a number of dissimilar network interfaces and dissimilar types of network interfaces (1 Gb or 10 Gb Ethernet) that are available

- The ESXi server design regulates the redundancy that we can offer for network communication

- The ESXi server design should include components that are required to be considered, such as blade server or rack-mounted server, which will shake the overall network topology

- The ESXi server design should include components that are required to be considered, such as chipset architecture, which will shake the PCIe slot performance

As we can see, quite a few factors have a great impact on our network design. In some scenarios, these influences might really push the design in deviating directions! It's up to the virtualization architect to resolve these factors with functional and nonfunctional requirements, restraints, and hazards as you build the network design.

Designing a vSphere network

After understanding the design of VSS and VDS, it is now time to read about designing a network for the virtual datacenter, aligning to design framework factors that need to be considered, such as availability, performance, management, and recoverability.

Readiness

When we design our network infrastructure and iron out a single point of failure, always consider high availability, including two switches, two routers, two NICs for the ESXi host, and two power supplies. The readiness of our design should focus on traffic, such as management traffic, IP storage, applications, VM, IP-based storage, vMotion and fault tolerance traffic. You can use the following techniques to accommodate the aforementioned factors:

- Make sure that your design uses multiple physical NIC ports on ESXi.

- Make sure that your design uses multiple physical switches on your network.

- Make sure that your design uses physical switches that are itself as resilient as likely.

- Make sure that your operational aspects are considered. Your teams should be skilled enough to handle a virtualized datacenter.

Performance

When we design our infrastructure, there would be a 10 GB Ethernet NIC for your organization network management stack, alternative for resilience, two for IP storage, and some other for VMs and vMotion. Consider the following components for optimal performance across your design:

- Management network
- ESXi NIC vMotion
- ESXi NIC for IP storage
- Virtual Machine vSwitch and vNICs

Management

When we design our infrastructure, we can replicate two major zones to make sure that the network is as controllable as possible . Both of these zones fall under the operational phase of the vSphere design:

- A management pane is required for a remote administrator to manage devices
- Naming standards and IP reservation

Recoverability

To make sure that the design of the network is capable of recovering on its own, we should consider the following:

- Backups of the network device configurations and setting an interval threshold for the backups
- Setting up a standard technique for scripts that can effortlessly recreate the vSwitch configuration in exactly the same way as it was previously
- Periodically documenting all the changes that are made to our infrastructure
- Creating a procedure and process to best meet the preceding requirements

It is worth considering the preceding essentials and recommendations on our design. In the next section, we will see the maximum configuration that is allowed in vSphere 5.5.

Network configuration limits

The following limits represent the achievable maximum configuration limits for networking in an infrastructure:

Component	Configuration
For physical NIC, this is the number of e1000e 1 Gb Ethernet ports	24
For physical NIC, this is the number of igb 1 Gb Ethernet	16
For physical NIC, this is the number of tg3 1 Gb Ethernet	32
For physical NIC, this is the number of bnx2 1 Gb Ethernet	16
For physical NIC, this is the number of nx_nic 10 Gb Ethernet ports	8
For physical NIC, this is the number of be2net 10 Gb Ethernet ports (Serverengines)	8
For physical NIC, this is the number of ixgbe 10 Gb Ethernet ports	8
For physical NIC, this is the number of bnx2x 10 Gb Ethernet ports	8
For physical NIC, this is the number of Infinib and ports	1
For physical NIC, this is the number of combinations of 10 Gb and 1 Gb Ethernet ports maximum can be configured	Eight 10 Gb and four 1 Gb ports
For physical NIC, this is the number of mlx4_en 40 Gb Ethernet ports	4
For VMDirectPath, this is the number of VMDirectPath PCI/PCIe devices per ESXi host	8
For VMDirectPath, this is the number of SR-IOV Number of virtual functions	64
For VMDirectPath, this is the number of SR-IOV Number of 10 G pNICs	8
For VMDirectPath, this is the number of of VMDirectPath PCI/ PCIe devices per VM	4
Total number of virtual network switch ports per host (VDS and VSS Ports)	4096
Total number of maximum active ports per host (VDS and VSS)	1016
Total number amount of virtual network switch creation ports per standard switch	4088
Total number of port groups per standard switch	512
Total number of static/dynamic port groups per distributed switch	6500
Total number of ephemeral port groups per distributed switch	1016
Total number of ports per distributed switch	60000
Total number of distributed virtual network switch ports per vCenter	60000

Component	Configuration
Total number of static/dynamic port groups per vCenter	10000
Total number of ephemeral port groups per vCenter	1016
Total number of distributed switches per vCenter	128
Total number of distributed switches per ESXi host	16
Total number of VSS port groups per ESXi host	1000
Total number of LACP-LAGs per ESXi host	64
Total number of LACP Uplink ports per LAG (Team)	32
Total number of hosts per distributed	1000
Total number of NetIOC resource pools per VDS	64
Total number of link aggregation groups per VDS maximum can be configured	64

Here, the VM traffic drives via vSwitch 1, and vSwitch 0 grips management traffic on vmnic 0, followed by vMotion on vmnic 1. On vSwitch 2, IP storage goes through vmnic 4, and FT goes through vmnic 5. Take a look at the following diagram:

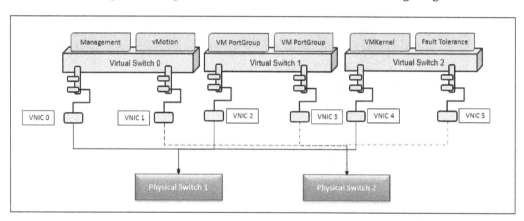

We have resilience for all modules, but the FT and IP storage traffic should have only one vNIC respectively. Based on your sizing of the virtual environment, this power may not provide enough, hence size it properly according your requirements.

Design considerations for networks with industry inputs

Here are some of the key design considerations followed worldwide by experts. Consider using some of them:

- Ensuring that vMotion and FT traffic are encrypted in your design; if not, it will result in security breach.

- Planning whether to use Microsoft NLB in your design or not. It's a decent awareness to select "No" to inform switches about VM MAC discourse deviations.

- Considering whether to include VM sizing and functionality into a version when sizing your vMotion network.

- Choosing to opt for a NIC that chains jumbo frames, NetQueue and TCP, and checksum offload to boost your design and achieve better performance.

- Limiting and sharing Network I/O Control in your design.

- Choosing a route-based policy on physical NIC load balancing in your design.

- Using a virtual infrastructure, such as vShield App, in your design. This will segregate DMZ traffic from the production network, provided this is sanctioned by the corporate security policy.

- Using 1 Gb Ethernet in your design. We must have minimum of one supplementary NIC to accompaniment the onboard NICs for resilience and feast groups across them.

- Using VDS in your design with the NFS/iSCSI option set and vMotion traffic on separate active uplinks.

- Using antimalware security in your VMs design. VMware recommends using the **vShield Endpoint solution**.

- Using VDS in your design. Make sure that the vMotion and NFS/iSCSI traffic has been routed via dedicated active physical uplinks for traffic.

- Using many dual or quad 1 Gb NIC in the VMware ESXi host; this is for the very purpose of isolating the physical NICS for each vSwitch on varied cards.

- Using active or additional uplink formations on your port groups if in case we need to isolate traffic while utilizing the VDS.

- In your design, if you plan use a multi-NIC vMotion formations on your cluster, each of the VMkernel interfaces contributing in the vMotion should have the IP addresses to the similar IP subnet.

- In your design, if you plan to use two 10 GB network adaptors, use a VDS with NetIOC and form the boundaries and dividends for the dissimilar traffic to consume.

- Considering the availability of numerous physical NIC ports as a portion of a one vSwitch.

- Using the Promiscuous mode for IPS. It's better to design a distinct vSwitch and relate it to suitable policies.

- Using port channels in a virtual environment and making sure that all NICs are active and belong to the same port channel.

Summary

In this chapter, you read about the VMware vSphere Networking essentials, the design of VMware vSphere standard and distributed switches, factors that influence virtual networks, the design of VMware vSphere Network, and design considerations for the management layer with industry inputs. In the next chapter, you will learn how to design VMware vSphere Storage.

4
Designing VMware vSphere Storage

A virtual datacenter has a number of critical mechanisms, and storage is a major part of any datacenter or design. It is the axiomatic essence of every virtual infrastructure. Without a functioning storage infrastructure, the ability for VM to write data and operate as you know it would impossible.

VMware vSphere brings many new capabilities that extend the benefits of vSphere, including a number of new, storage-related features and enhancements that also bring additional scalability and performance capabilities. This chapter focuses on storage-specific design essentials, designing vSphere storage, and design considerations with various industry inputs.

In this chapter, we will cover the following topics:

- VMware vSphere storage essentials
- Determining factors that influence vSphere storage
- Designing vSphere storage
- Configuration considerations for better vSphere storage design
- Design considerations for storage layers with industry inputs

VMware vSphere storage essentials

VMware ESXi provides storage virtualization based on the ESXi host (this logically abstracts the datacenter storage layer from VM and ESXi) whereas VM uses a virtual disk to store its OS, program files, and other data associated with its activities. A virtual disk is a small-to-big physical file that can be moved, copied, backed up, and archived effortlessly. We are permitted to configure the VM with as many virtual disks as it supports. In order to access virtual disks, a VM uses virtual SCSI controllers, such as **BusLogic Parallel**, **LSI Logic SAS**, **LSI Logic Parallel**, and **VMware Paravirtual**. These controllers are the only types of SCSI controllers that a VM can see and access.

Before we dive deep into the essentials of VMware vSphere, let's explore VMware storage terminologies. Physical servers attach directly to the storage, either internal to the server chassis or in an exterior array.

About data store and VM associations; VM is stored as a set of files in its own directory in a data store. It is a logical container, like a filesystem, that hides the specifics of each storage device and provides a uniform model to store VM files. Data stores can also be used to store VM templates, ISO images, and floppy images, which can be backed by either a VMFS or a network filesystem, based on the type of storage.

About VMFS; VMware vSphere VMFS allows multiple vSphere ESXi hosts to access the shared VM storage concurrently and enables virtualization-based distributed architecture to operate across a cluster of vSphere ESXi hosts. They provide the basis for scaling virtualization outside its limitations, and VMware vSphere supports all common storage interconnects for block-based storage, including direct-attached storage, **Fiber Channel (FC)**, **FCoE (Fiber Channel over Ethernet)**, and iSCSI. VMware vSphere also supports placing data stores on NAS storage, accessed via an IP network, and the following table illustrates networked storage technologies that VMware ESXi supports:

Technology	Protocols	Transfers	Interface
Fiber Channel	FC/SCSI	Block access of data/LUN	FC HBA
NAS	IP/NFS	File	Network adapter
iSCSI	IP/SCSI	Block access of data/LUN	Hardware iSCSI and software iSCSI
Fiber Channel over Ethernet	FCoE/ SCSI	Block access of data/LUN	Hardware FCoE and software FCoE

The following table illustrates the VMware vSphere features that different types of storage support:

Storage Type	BootVM	RDM	VM Cluster	vMotion	Data store	HA and DRS
Local Storage	Yes	No	Yes	No	VMFS	No
NAS over NFS	Yes	No	No	Yes	NFS	Yes
iSCSI	Yes	Yes	Yes	Yes	VMFS	Yes
Fiber Channel	Yes	Yes	Yes	Yes	VMFS	Yes

Now, let's explore VMware vSphere storage essentials in greater depth. The virtual disk resides on a data store that is positioned on physical storage. From the standpoint of the VM, each virtual disk appears as if it were a SCSI drive connected to a SCSI controller. Regardless of whether the actual physical storage is being read through, the storage on the ESXi host is classically transparent to the guest OS that runs on the VM; moreover, on top of virtual disks VMware vSphere offers a contrivance called **raw device mapping**. It is applicable when a guest operation system inside a VM requires direct access to a storage device.

VMware vSphere storage architecture comprises three layers of abstraction that hide alterations and accomplish complexity among physical storage components:

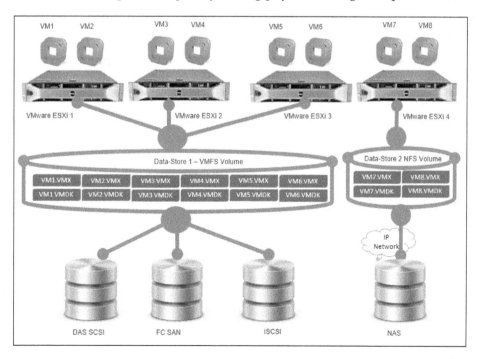

VMware infrastructure enables world-class storage performance, functionality, and availability, without adding complexity to the user applications and guest OS.

The data store provides a modest model to allocate storage space for the individual VMs without exposing them to difficulties caused by the variety of physical storage technologies available, such as iSCSI SAN, Fiber Channel SAN, DAS, and NAS.

A data store is nothing but a physical VMFS filesystem volume or a directory on a NAS. Each data store can span numerous physical storage components. As illustrated in the preceding diagram, one VMFS volume can encompass one or more LUNs from a DAS SCSI disk array on a physical machine, iSCSI SAN disk farm, or a Fiber Channel SAN disk farm. New LUNs added to any of the physical storage components are automatically discovered and made accessible to ESXi; this can be added to extend a previously created data store without powering off the ESXi servers or storage components. Conversely, if any of the LUNs within a data store are not working or have failed for some reason, only VMs that reside in the failed LUN are affected. The remaining VMs residing in other LUNs continue to work as they are.

VMFS is a clustered filesystem that can influence shared storage to permit numerous physical ESXi hosts to read and write to the same storage concurrently. VMFS provides mechanisms that can lock on a disk; it isolates it to make sure that the same VM is not switched on by multiple ESXi hosts at the same time. If a physical ESXi host fails, the on-disk lock for each VM can be released so that VMs can be restarted on other physical ESXi hosts.

VMFS provides support for raw device mapping. Raw device mapping can be viewed as a symbolic link from a VMFS volume to a raw LUN. It makes LUNs look like files in a VMFS volume. The mapping file, not the raw LUN, is referenced in the VM.

When a LUN is opened for access, VMFS resolves the RDM file to the correct physical device and performs appropriate access checks and locking. Thereafter, reads/writes go directly to the raw LUN rather than going through the mapping file.

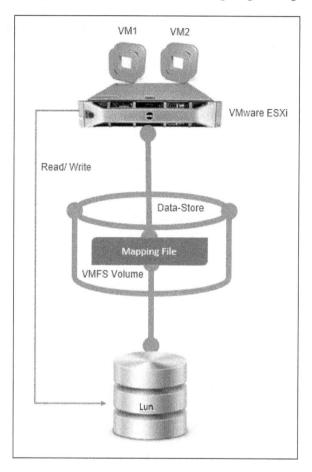

This is referenced in the VM configuration. Using RDMs, we can use vMotion to migrate VMs using raw LUNs, add raw LUNs to VMs using the vSphere Web Client, and use filesystem features, such as distributed file locking, permissions, and naming.

The following are the compatibility modes that are available for RDMs:

- Virtual compatibility mode permits an RDM to act accurately like a virtual disk file
- Physical compatibility mode permits direct access to the SCSI device for applications that need low-level control

Determining factors that influence vSphere storage

Over the years, people designed and built servers and paid more money for server storage. These physical servers used local direct DAS, with the infrequent raid into two node clusters, with limited performance. When businesses were in need of greater performance, they scaled out with multiple servers, or some businesses bought expensive, dedicated Fiber Channel SAN with influential array technologies. This has changed a lot with the advent of virtualization; storage is now much more than just its own capacity. Arguably, the number of terabytes that our new storage array can provide is a relatively minor interest when we are investigating requirements.

Now let's explore the factors that need to be considered, such as hard disk, performance over capacity, IOPS, and spindle considerations.

Hard disks

The following guidelines will help you in identifying the influencing factors between shared storage and local storage:

- Clustering of VMs across ESXi hosts
- Central repository that is accessible from multiple ESXi hosts
- Data replication and scalable and recoverable rollouts
- Using VMware vMotion, HA, DRS, and DPM

Performance

Performance is mostly less understood than capacity or availability but, in a virtualized infrastructure where there is substantial scope for alliance, it has a much greater influence. We can use numerous metrics—such as IOPS, throughput, and latency—to accurately measure performance.

Capacity

Capacity needs to be achieved on an ongoing basis as a business grows or shrinks, and it is generally predicted and provisioned on-demand though, unlike availability and performance, it can normally be augmented as requirements grow. It's a relatively easy procedure to add disks and enclosures to most storage arrays without experiencing downtime. So, we can normally solve capacity issues relatively easily, but it is worth considering this factor on your design.

IOPS

Workload is a crucial consideration when designing for optimal performance. Workload is characterized by IOPS, and write versus read percentages. Optimal design is usually used to determine how many IOPs you can achieve with a given number of disks. The formula behind this factor involves the Total RAW IOPS and Functional RAW IOPS.

Use the following formula to calculate Total RAW IOPS:

Total Raw IOPS = Disk IOPS * Number of disks

Use the following formula to calculate Functional IOPS:

Functional IOPS = (Raw IOPS * Write %)/(Raid Penalty) + (Raw IOPS * Read %)

The number of disks that are required to achieve a required IOPS value is the next factor that needs to be identified:

Disks Required = ((Read IOPS) + (Write IOPS*Raid Penalty))/ Disk IOPS

Spindles

Consider using SSD, which potentially removes the physical limitation of spinning media.

Cost

The budget that we want to spend will depend. It might be a large number, and we can think of it as a design constraint. As an alternative, your design needs to focus on system readiness, performance, and capacity. We must design a world-class solution with the future in mind, regardless of the expense.

Usually, the task of a decent design is to take in the necessities and provide the best solution for the lowest conceivable cost. Even if we aren't accountable for the financial aspects of the design, it's useful to have an impression of how much money is offered.

We know that the above listed factors are not comprehensive, as we are only discussing design essentials; you can add you are own factors whenever required. In the next section, let's discuss designing storage.

Designing vSphere storage

In a virtual datacenter, storage is a serious subject that is often disregarded. In a faultless business world, a virtualization project should be given unlimited cost and a clean slate to achieve what the business wants from storage. However, if we do not have a clean slate or an unlimited budget and, often, if you have been asked to use an already existing SAN, most virtual datacenters will have a SAN infrastructure implemented around a favored storage vendor's product family.

In this section, let's talk about the different types of storage available to VMware vSphere virtualization. Let's begin with FC. FC is a gold standard for both performance and connectivity, with speeds from 1 Gbps to 2 Gbps, 4 Gbps, 8 Gbps, and 16 Gbps. Initially, it was designed, as the name suggests, to use fiber optic cabling. In the past years, the standard has permitted the use of copper cabling. FC was designed to provide access to disks or storage. FC is typically implemented through a switch, a couple of switches, or director. Switches are classically smaller semimodular, less-redundant devices to support the storage infrastructure, whereas directors consist of a high port count and modular slot-based chassis, with more resilient switches, hosts, adapters, and the storage associated together to form a fabric.

Design-leveraging FC, while often complex and classy, provides high levels of readiness and performance that rely on our business requirements. This may be the best solution.

VMware ESXi supports different storage systems and arrays. The types of storage that our host supports include active-active, active-passive, and ALUA-compliant:

Fiber Channel Storage Array Types	Capabilities
Active-active storage system	Features permit access to the LUNs instantaneously through all the storage ports that are accessible without important performance degradation. All the paths are active at all times, unless a path loses communication.

Fiber Channel Storage Array Types	Capabilities
Active-passive storage system	Features that permit access to the system in which one storage processor is aggressively providing access to a given LUN. The other processors act as backups for the LUN and can aggressively provide access to other LUN I/Os. I/Os can be effectively sent only to an active port for a given LUN. If sending through the active storage port fails, one of the passive storage processors can be stimulated by the servers to retrieve it.
Asymmetrical storage system	Features support **Asymmetric Logical Unit Access (ALUA)**. ALUA-complaint storage systems offer different levels of admittance per port. ALUA allows hosts to regulate the states of target ports and rank paths. The ESXi host uses some of the active paths as primary and others as secondary.

Next, let's discuss iSCSI, which is nothing but the Internet Small Computer Systems Interface protocol. It has been used since the days before x86 virtualization. One cool VMware feature in ESXi is a software adapter that permits us to access our storage via our available NIC without having to make investments in additional NIC, if we have a limited budget. However, hardware is more effective and can provide a fabric similar to FC-leveraging dedicated Ethernet adapters or converged network adapters.

Another benefit related with iSCSI is the capability to go above and beyond traditional Ethernet networking and provide 10 GbE connectivity to vSphere infrastructures. A dedicated network for our core virtual infrastructure is a must-do. The following are some considerations to prevent issues. When using ESXi in conjunction with a SAN, we must follow specific guidelines to avoid SAN problems:

- Multiple VMFS data stores on one LUN are not recommended; hence, place only one VMFS data store on each LUN

- Never change the path policy the machine sets unless you know the inferences of making such a change

- Consider these options in the event of disaster or failure:

  - Make several copies of your topology maps. Consider what happens to your SAN if any of the elements fails.

  - Cross off different links, switches, HBAs and other elements to ensure we did not miss a critical loss point in our design.

iSCSI storage that our ESXi host supports includes active-active, active-passive, and ALUA compliant and its capabilities are illustrated in following table.

Fiber Channel Storage Array Types	Capabilities
Active-active storage system	Features permits access to the LUNs concurrently through all the storage ports that are obtainable without noteworthy performance degradation. All the paths are active at all times, unless a path lost communication.
Active-passive storage system	Features aid the system in which one storage processor is aggressively providing permission to a given LUN. The other processors act as backup for the LUN and can be aggressively providing access to other LUN I/O. I/O can be effectively sent only to an active port for a given LUN.
Asymmetrical storage system	Features support Asymmetric Logical Unit Access. ALUA-complaint storage devices provide different levels of access per port. ALUA permits ESXi hosts to regulate the states of target ports and prioritize paths. The ESXi host uses some of the active paths as primary while others as secondary.
Virtual port storage system	Features permit access to all obtainable LUNs through one virtual port. These are active-active storage devices, but for their multiple connections through one port. ESXi multipath does not make multiple communications from a specific port to the storage. Some storage manufactures supply session managers to found and manage manifold communication to their storage. These storage systems handle port failover and communication balancing clearly. This is also called **transparent failover**.

The next storage that we will discuss is FCoE. FCoE engages some of the flexibility of iSCSI with the competencies of the Fiber Channel protocol's importance-based flow control, among other competencies.

The design decision to adopt FCoE over traditional FC or iSCSI is often expected to reduce the adapters required to connect to storage and IP networks and reduce the number of cables routing from ESXi host to switches. This in turns reduces cooling costs and power consumption, and it is best to adopt the following conditions into your design:

- On the ports that communicate with an ESXi host, disable the Spanning Tree Protocol. Having the STP enabled might delay the FCoE Initialization Protocol response at the switch and cause the path failure state.

- Priority-based Flow Control should be turned on and configured to AUTO.

- Ensure that firmware such as Cisco Nexus 5000 (version 4.1(3)N2 or higher) and Brocade FCoE switch (version 6.3.1 or higher) on the FCoE switch are applied.

- If we plan to enable software FCoE adapters to work with network adapters, the following facts should be considered:
    - Ensure that the newest microcode is deployed on the FCOE network adapter
    - If the network adapter has multiple ports, while configuring networking add each port to a separate vSwitch; this will avoid an APD condition when a disruptive event occurs
    - Never consider the option to move the network adapter port from one vSwitch to another when FCOE traffic is active

The final storage type that we will be discussing is NFS. NFS was established as a network filesystem for UNIX to permit access to network files in the same way as if they were local ones. NFS is arguably the most cost-effective and the simplest to manage. Some storage suppliers even enhance deduplication on NFS to reduce the virtual footprint.

Before NFS storage can be addressed by an ESX server, the following issues need to be addressed:

- Ensure that the virtual switch is configured for IP-based storage
- VMware ESXi hosts need to be configured to enable their own NFS clients
- The NFS storage server needs to be configured in order to export a mount point that is accessible to the ESXi host over a trusted network

The default setting for the maximum number of mount point data stores an ESX server can concurrently mount is eight. Although the limit can be increased to 64 in the latest release, if you increase the maximum NFS mounts above eight, make sure that you increase `Net.TcpipHeapSize` as well.

The following table will help you know which storage is accurate for your design:

Components to be considered	iSCSI	NFS	Fiber Channel	FCoE
ESXi Boot from SAN	Yes	No	Yes	No - SW FCoE Yes - HW FCoE
RDM Support	Yes	No	Yes	Yes
Maximum Device Size	64 TB	64 TB, but requires NAS vendor to support it	64 TB	64 TB
ESXi Boot from SAN	Yes	No	Yes	No for SW FCoE Yes for HW FCoE/CAN
Maximum number of devices	256	Default 8 to maximum 256	256	256
Protocol direct to VM	Yes, only via guest iSCSI initiator	Yes, only via guest NFS client	No	No
Storage vMotion Support	Yes	Yes	Yes	Yes
Storage DRS Support	Yes	Yes	Yes	Yes
Storage I/O Control Support	Yes, since vSphere 4.1	Yes, since vSphere 5.0	Yes, since vSphere 4.1	Yes, since vSphere 4.1
Load Balancing	VMware PSA/MPIO	Non-single Session	VMware PSA/MPIO	VMware PSA/MPIO
High Availability	VMware PSA via SATP	NIC teaming	VMware PSA via SATP	VMware PSA via SATP
VAAI Support	Yes	No	Yes	Yes
vMSC	Yes	Yes	Yes	Yes
SRM	Yes	Yes	Yes	Yes

As you have now read about the different types of storage, let's start by designing accurate storage for our virtual infrastructure. Answering the following will provide us with the best storage for our requirements:

- Identify the storage protocol — NFS, Fiber Chancel, or iSCSI — of your choice
- Identity the mode of deployment of ESXi
- Identify the commodity servers or a converged solution
- Identify the number of HBAs we need per ESXi host
- Identify the sort of controllers and disk that will be purchased, based on what we need our storage to do
- Identify whether we have the necessary hardware redundancy for FT (necessary means having multiple CNAs, HBAs, or NICs per ESXi host, multiple paths, and connections to multiple redundant switches)
- Identify the capacity requirement for the present and future
- Identify designing for capacity, meaning RAID option considerations, VMFS capacity limits, array compression, and data deduplication.
- Identify designing for performance — in other words, measuring storage performance against requirements and calculating a disk IOPS against the VM/application requirements.
- Identify the right model storage, meaning local storage or shared storage (we'll go into this in greater detail in the following section)
- Ensure you meet the demands of integration, such as high performance, availability, and efficiency
- Make sure that you avoid using extents to grow VMFS
- Make sure that you use PVSCSI controllers whenever demanded
- Make sure that you use jumbo frames for iSCSI/NFS
- Make sure that you always isolate network storage traffic
- Make sure that you always read the vendor best practices for your array design
- Identify the point at which the total guest latency measure arrives in storage devices: KAVG (the amount of time IOPS spent on VMkernel), queue latency (the amount of time IOPS spent in HBA driver), and device latency (the amount of time IOPS spent in leaving HBA)

Storage considerations

In this section, let's explore shared storage against local storage. Shared storage, which is nothing but SAN or NAS devices, has become so common in vSphere implementation that local storage is often not considered to be an option at all. It's certainly true that each new release of VMware's vSphere products provides greater functionality for shared storage. However, local storage has its place and can offer tangible advantages. Each design is different and needs to be loomed only with focus on requirement; never dismiss local storage before you identify the real needs of your design.

Local storage versus shared storage

Local storage or DAS means the disks from which we intend to run the VMs mounted as VMFS data stores. These disks can be physically attached to the ESXi hosts. The disks can also be in a distinct enclosure connected via a SCSI cable to an external-facing SCSI card's connector. Even if outwardly mounted, it's logically still local host storage for ESXi.

Note that there are sure advantages from shared storage. The following are some points to consider as essentials against design:

- Though there are huge enhancements in vSphere 5.1 and as shared storage is no longer an obligation for vMotion, **Distributed Resource Scheduler (DRS)** will not use VMs local storage.

- High-availability-enabled ESXi hosts need to have access to VMs in order to recover them when a protected ESXi host fails.

- Fault tolerance-enabled ESXi hosts need a secondary ESXi host to access the same VM so that it can step in if the primary ESXI host fails.

- If you have planned to use shared storage in your design, you can recover from host failures far more easily. If you're using local storage and a server fails for some reason, the VMs will be offline until the server can be brought online. With shared storage, even without the use of HA, we can restart the VMs on another ESXi host.

- Local storage capacity is imperfect in several respects, counting the size of the SCSI enclosures and the number of SCSI connectors and data stores.

- Using shared storage, it's possible to have a joint store for ISOs and templates. On the other hand, if you use local storage, each ESXi host needs to retain its own copy of each template.

- Using shared storage for ESXi, we can run ESXi diskless servers that can boot from SAN. This successfully makes the ESXi hosts stateless, additionally reducing implementation overheads.

- We can also use local storage for VM's swap files, which, in turn, can save more space than on shared storage for VMs. However, this method can have an effect on DRS and HA if there isn't adequate space on the destination ESXi hosts to get the migrated VMs.

- The technical blockade for deploying local storage is very low slung in comparison to the challenge of configuring a new SAN fabric or NAS devices.

- Local storage is regularly in place for the ESXi-installable OS. This means that there is regularly local space offered for VMFS data stores, or it's moderately simple to add extra disks to procure new servers.

In a nutshell, shared storage is the cornerstone of most Enterprise vSphere rollouts. Local storage originated in small business vSphere rollouts, where businesses were new to the concept or lacked the budget. To take full advantage of VMware vSphere and all it has to offer, a shared storage explanation is the comprehensible first choice. Shared storage highlights the primary goals that your design should focus on. Here are the following components that align to the PPP approach:

- Shared storage readiness generates superior redundancy and reliability and lessens failure.

- Shared storage performance means better I/O performance and scalability. Superior disk spindles, powerful controllers with large read/write cache options, and tiers of dissimilar storage disks all result in better performance.

- Shared storage capacity assembles storage, permits the use of progressive capacity-reduction knowhow, and can speech huge amounts of stowage space.

Storage DRS provides intelligent VM placement and load-balancing mechanisms based on I/O latency and storage capacity. Here are the benefits of placing storage in the SDRS mode:

- Improve service levels by guaranteeing appropriate resources to VMs

- Deploy new capacity to a cluster without service disruption

- Automatically migrate VMs during maintenance without service disruption

- Monitor and manage more infrastructure per system administrator

VMware vSphere DRS is a feature included in the vSphere Enterprise and Enterprise Plus editions.

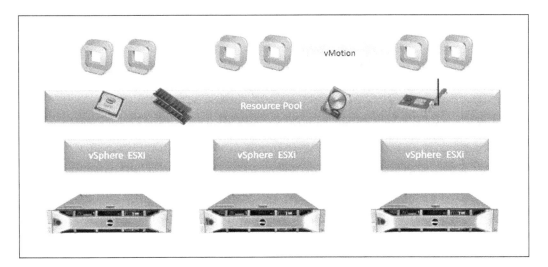

Provisioning is often overlooked. It is worth considering this option in your design. The upcoming tables illustrate three different methods; by default, ESXi offers a traditional storage provisioning method called **thick provisioning** for VM. With this method, we first determine the amount of storage that VM will need for its entire life cycle existences. We then provision an immovable amount of storage space to VM well in advance.

For example, if you plan to allocate 40 GB, once this is allocated, we have the entire provisioned space committed to the VM's virtual disk. A virtual disk immediately occupies the entire provisioned space allocated to it; this is said to be thick provisioning and the latest version of ESXi also supports thin provisioning for VMs virtual disks. With the disk-level thin provisioning feature, we can create VM virtual disks in a thin format.

For a thin virtual disk, ESXi provisions the entire space required for the disk's current and future activities. Let's say, for example, that we want to allocate **40 GB**. A thin disk uses only as much storage space as it needs for its initial operations. In this example, the thin-provisioned disk occupies only **20 GB** of storage for its initial operations. As the disk requires more space, it can spread into its entire **40 GB** allocated space:

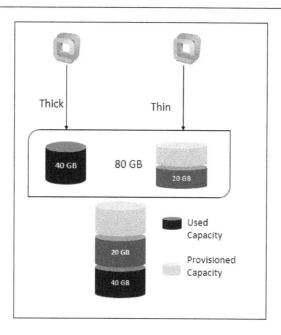

Thin provisioning is a technique that enhances storage utilization by assigning storage space in a flexible on-demand method. Thin provisioning is different from the traditional thick provisioning. With thick provisioning, a large quantity of storage space is provided on loan in expectation of future storage needs. However, the space might remain unused causing underutilization of storage. The following table explains the difference between three methods for a quick recap:

Provisioning method	Description
Thick Provision Eager Zero	In this type of provisioning, blocks are permitted and zeroed on provisioning. This is important when provisioning a fault-tolerant VM. This provisioning process takes longer as blocks are permitted and zeroed when creating the VMDK. This improves the first-time write performance.
Thick Provision Lazy Zero	In this type of provisioning, blocks are permitted upon creation but not zeroed until the VM first writes to the VMDK. This process happens quickly in comparison to an eager zero. Blocks are allocated, but space isn't used until the VM needs to write beyond the initial footprint.
Thin Provisioned	In this type of provisioning, we only use as much space as required by the initial write. We cannot convert to a thin-provisioned disk, but we can perform a storage vMotion to a thin-provisioned disk.

Raw device mapping

Worth considering in your design is raw device mapping. An RDM is a mapping file in a separate VMFS volume that acts as a proxy for a raw physical storage device. The RDM permits a VM to straightaway access the storage device.

The RDM comprises metadata to manage and send disk access to the physical device and RDM compatibility modes are available in the following two formats:

- The **virtual compatibility mode** permits an RDM to act accurately like a virtual disk file, counting the use of snapshots

- The **physical compatibility mode** permits direct access to the SCSI device for those applications that demand lower-level control

The following illustrates the limitations of using RDM in your design:

- We are not allowed to map to a disk partition. RDMs require the mapped device to be a whole LUN.

- If you have planned to use vMotion in order to migrate VMS with RDMs, ensure that you uphold steady LUN IDs for RDMs through all the contributing ESXi hosts.

- Flash Read Cache never supports RDMs in physical compatibility mode, whereas virtual compatibility RDMs support it.

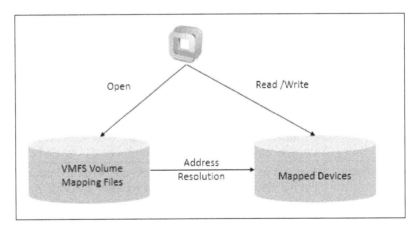

Virtual SAN

In your design, it is worth considering virtual SAN, which is nothing but a distributed layer of software that runs traditionally as a part of the ESXi host. Virtual SAN collects local or DAS disks of an ESXi host cluster and makes a single storage pool shared across all ESXi hosts of the cluster, and Virtual SAN removes the need for an external shared storage and shortens the storage formation and VM provisioning task.

vSAN virtualizes local physical storage resources assigned to ESXi hosts and converts them into resource pools of storage that can be assigned to the VM; this makes sure applications get the best out of it. Another great feature is when you make a vSAN cluster that does not require to be identical. Even ESXi hosts that have no local disks can participate and run their VMs on the Virtual SAN data store.

vSAN offers a significantly lower TCO by dropping CapEx and OpEx. Moreover, the product takes advantage of system-side hardware costs by combining interior magnetic disks and flash devices from x86 systems. Right from the start, and adding disks or nodes to their vSAN cluster as volume or performance requirements demand, organizations avoid big upfront charges. VSAN also helps organizations realize OpEx savings using automation, in turn eliminating manual procedures as well as easing usually complex change management, capacity planning tasks, and storage configuration.

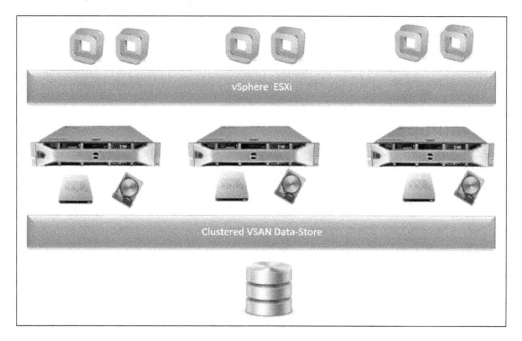

The following highpoints illustrate the limitations of using vSAN on your design:

- VSAN is deployed straight into the ESXi host, and it supports only SAS HDD, SATA, and PCIe storage
- VSAN does not support storage attached through Fiber Channel, iSCSI, and USB
- VSAN does not support multiple vSAN clusters for each ESXi host, VMs with only 2 TB and not more than that
- vSAN supports features such as HA, vMotion, and DRS
- VSAN does not support features such as FT, DPM, and Storage I/O Control
- VSAN does not support SE sparse disks, SCSI reservations, RDM, VMFS, diagnostic partition, and other disk-access features

Multipathing

In order to have high availability in your design as well as to maintain constant communication between an ESXi host and storage to which it is associated, VMware ESXi supports multipathing. Multipathing is nothing but a protocol that lets us use more than one physical path to transfer data between the ESXi host and storage to which it is associated. The main purpose is that—in the event of any failure of SAN components, such as a cable, adapter, or switch—VMware ESXi can switch over to another physical path that is designed to not use the failed component. This procedure of path switching to avoid using any of the failed components is known as **path failover** and, as an additional feature, multipathing also provides a load-balancing mechanism. Load balancing distributes I/O loads across multiple physical paths. It should be designed in such a way that it reduces or removes probable bottlenecks.

SAN multipathing

Using SAN FC multipathing local storage topology, in your design you can use one ESXi host with two HBAs. The ESXi host communicates with a dual-port local storage system through cables. This ESXi configuration aids FT if any one of the communication elements between the ESXi host and the local storage system fails.

In SAN FC multipathing, multiple paths attach the ESXi host to the storage device, as illustrated in following diagram:

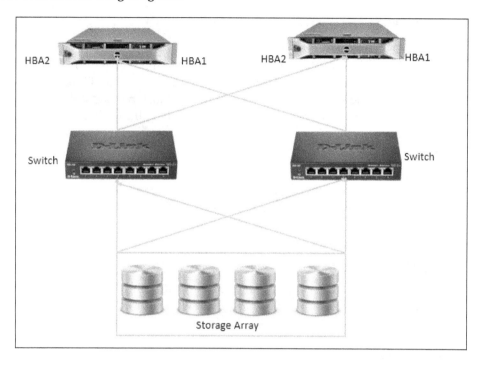

For example, if **HBA1** or the link between **HBA1** and the switch fails, then the network fails over to **HBA2**, and **HBA2** provides the communication between the ESXi host and the physical switch.

From the standpoint of VMware vSphere features, SAN multipathing is categorized into two groups:

- **Active-active**: This array can accept I/Os from all LUNs on all of their SPs instantaneously, without degrading performance; every path is active.

- **Active-passive**: This array permits only one SP to accept I/O for each LUN, using other SPs for failover. SPs can be dynamic for some LUNs, while they are standbys for others. Hence, all SPs can be active instantaneously.

With active-active arrays in your design, pick the active path on a LUN-by-LUN basis; this is often said to be fixed. For active -passive arrays, the ESXi hosts determine the active path themselves; this is often described as MRU.

Native multipathing plugin

VMware vSphere's latest feature presents a redesigned storage layer. VMware says that this has a **Pluggable Storage Architecture** (**PSA**). VMware has fragmented it into two discrete modules, which are as follows:

- **Storage Array Type Plugin (SATP)**: This is designed for path failover. The ESXi host recognizes the type of array and links the SATP based on its brand and model. The array's particulars are tartan against the ESXi host's /etc/vmware/esx.conf file, which will list all the HCL-certified storage arrays. This specifies whether the array is confidential as active-active or active-passive.

- **Path Selection Plugin (PSP)**: This is designed for load balancing and path selection. The native PSP has three types of path policy: fixed, MRU, Round-robin. These policies are robotically nominated on a per-LUN basis based on the SATP.

NAS multipathing

NAS multipathing is essentially dissimilar to SAN multipathing in VMware vSphere, because it depends on the networking stack. IP-based redundancy and routing are used. For each NFS export mounted by the ESXi host, only one physical NIC should be considered, notwithstanding any link-aggregation techniques used to intersect many composed NICs. NIC teaming offers failover redundancy but can't load balance an export. By making multiple exports along with many associates on different subnets, we can statically load spread data store traffic.

Now, we will design another essential by creating two or more vSwitches, each with a VMkernel interface, or a single vSwitch with more VMkernel uplinks. Each uplink communicates to a separate redundant physical switch. The VMkernel interfaces and NFS interfaces are split across different subnets, as illustrated in following diagram:

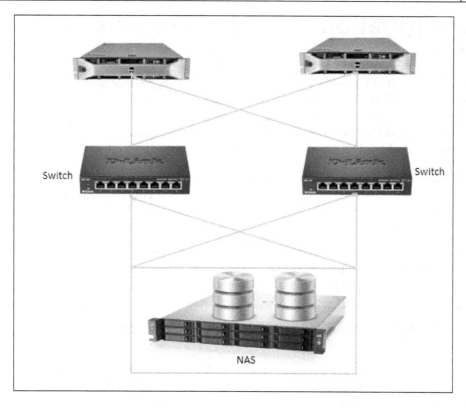

If you have considered in your design having physical switches that can cross-stack, then it is worth considering only one VMkernel interface. The NAS device requires multiple IP address targets. Plan your vSwitch with at least two NICs that are, in turn, split across the two cross-stacked switches. Ensure that VMkernel's vSwitch has its load-balancing NIC teaming policy enabled with route based on IP hash and, then, plan to combine the physical switch ports into an 802.3ad EtherChannel static option. Alternatively, if you are using a VDS, ensure that you use its dynamic LACP support to organize the EtherChannel. Also, plan to use round-robin DNS to mount the targets under different IP addresses.

Configuration considerations for better vSphere storage design

The ESXi hosts that we deploy and the amount of storage space that the VM requires regulate the level of service that we can provide in the environment and how well the environment can scale to higher service demands as the business grows. The list of factors we need to consider when building our virtual infrastructure so it scales in response to workload changes is as follows:

- Load balancing can be achieved using vMotion or VMware DRS to migrate a VM to other ESXi hosts for high availability. If you are planning to use shared storage in your design, we can design load balancing without any disruption to the business.

- Storage consolidation and simplifying storage layout helps consolidate storage resources to achieve benefits in a virtual infrastructure. We can start designing by reserving a large volume and then allowing portions to VM on demand.

- Disaster recovery is yet another option that needs to be considered when all the data is stored on a SAN. Importantly, this can enable remote storage of data backups.

In order to achieve the preceding two factors, it is worth considering the sizing option that is available from the VMware vSphere product itself. The following table illustrates the maximum configuration that should be considered on your design (never overcommit):

Virtual Disk	
Configuration	Maximum
Virtual Disks per ESXi host	2,048
iSCSI Physical	
LUNs per system	256
Qlogic 1 Gb iSCSI HBA initiator ports per ESXi host	4
Broadcom 1 Gb iSCSI HBA initiator ports per ESXi host	4
Broadcom 10 Gb iSCSI HBA initiator ports per ESXi host	4
NICs that can be associated or port-bound with the software iSCSI stack per ESXi host	8
Number of total paths on a server	1,024
Number of paths to a LUN	8
Qlogic iSCSI: dynamic targets per adapter port	64
Qlogic iSCSI: static targets per adapter port	62

Virtual Disk	
Configuration	**Maximum**
Broadcom 1 Gb iSCSI HBA targets per adapter port	641
Broadcom 10 Gb iSCSI HBA targets per adapter port	128
Software iSCSI targets	2,561
NAS	
NFS mounts per ESXi host	256
Fiber Channel	
LUNs per ESXi host	256
LUN size	64 TB
LUN ID	255
Number of paths to a LUN	32
Number of total paths on a server	1,024
Number of HBAs of any type	8
HBA ports	16
Targets per HBA	256
FCoE	
Software FCoE adapters	4
Common VMFS	
Volume size	64
Volumes per host	256
Hosts per volume	64
Powered on VMs per VMFS volume	2,048
Concurrent vMotion operations per VMFS volume	128
VMFS3	
Raw device mapping size (virtual and physical)	2 TB minus 512 bytes
Block size	8 MB
File size (1 MB block size)	256 GB
File size (2 MB block size)	512 GB
File size (4 MB block size)	1 TB
File size (8 MB block size)	2 TB minus 512 bytes
Files per volume approximately	30,720
VMFS5	
Raw Device Mapping size (virtual compatibility)	62 TB

Virtual Disk	
Configuration	Maximum
Raw Device Mapping size (physical compatibility)	64 TB
Block size	1 MB
File size	62 TB
Files per volume approximately	130,690

Design considerations of storage layers with industry inputs

Design consideration for storage should start with architecting VMware storage. It should follow the life cycle, starting with gathering and developing a technical specification; estimating cost, ROI, and TCO; developing high-level design for storage implementation; and following low-level considerations, such as IOPS, RAID, interface, controllers, cache, coalescing, storage workload catalog, storage alignment, and performance fine-tuning.

While designing your infrastructure, follow the PPP approach and the following key points will assist you further in creating a better design:

- Choose a requirement-based vendor for storage. Ensure that storage vendor supports advanced vSphere features, such as VAAI and VASA, if these components are considered in your design.

- Choose a homogenous or heterogeneous server and storage platform and identify whether in your design you have placed a blade or rack server, based on the identify protocol.

- In your design, always have scalability options such as scale-out at the edge of the core.

- In your design, always have backup and disaster recovery as mandatory components; it is worth considering the option of centralized disaster tolerances.

- In your design, if you have planned to use SAN, pick the right topologies; focus on resilience and redundancy.

- In your design, consider the data flow such as congestion in the fabric, traffic versus frame congestion, and bottleneck detection.

- In your design, it's recommended that you use SIOC and Storage DRS to achieve the assignment and performance of the (monster) VMs.

- In your design, if you are using an NFS data store as a persistent scratch or log location, mount it via IP; this will avoid DNS dependency.

- In your design, choose to create LUNs with adequate space to fit a bigger VMDK (up to 2 TB); keep the option open for flexibility.

- In your design, consider Storage DRS whenever autotiring is enabled on the disk system or whenever intelligent caching solutions are used. Make sure that the I/O metric option is disabled for better performance and optimization.

- In your design, consider storage infrastructure in the light of future capacity, performance, and business continuity.

- In your design, ensure that the storage performance comprehends that the coldness to storage and RAID type cast-off can have an impression on performance.

- In your design for VMware View solutions, ensure that you accurately support the early implementation, recompose, refresh, and rebalance processes with negligible impact to ESXi hosts and the disk system.

- If you have enabled design for VM clones and snapshots, consider storage arrays that support vStorage APIs. Hardware-accelerated clones and snapshots provide greater performance and scalability.

- Always use vCenter Plugins provided by the storage vendor for NFS data store.

- For active VMware VAAI functions in your storage design, ensure that all data stores have a matching block size; this will result in faster recital and efficient operations.

- In your design, if you are using multipathing FC for storage, consider using a single-initiator for zoning.

- In your design, to obtain better Storage I/O Control, apply to all data stores to share the same physical spindles; this in turn will create a performance issue, due to assigning the same spindles.

- On your design, make sure that the data stores are in a data store cluster placed on different physical disks; this, in turn, enables I/O and the capacity to be obtainable.

Summary

In this chapter, you read about VMware vSphere storage essentials, determining factors that influence vSphere storage, how to design vSphere Storage, configuration considerations for better vSphere storage design, and design consideration for storage layers with industry inputs. In the next chapter, we will learn how to design VMware vCloud.

5
Designing VMware vRealize

Today, the virtualization world faces many challenges in trying to respond to rapidly growing and ever-changing business environments on very limited budgets, requirements to support legacy applications, as well as new contemporary cloud applications and big data systems. An organization won't have enough money to start over and build applications for the cloud from scratch; to mitigate this particular problem, cloud computing provides an important solution in terms of quickness and cost efficiency. We can easily end up with workloads that can only run on premises and off premises (public cloud). Once you have chosen to move a workload to an exclusive cloud, you'll typically need to rewrite the application's source and reconfigure your infrastructure to move between public and private clouds.

In this chapter, you will learn about the following topics:

- Essentials of cloud computing
- Purposes of cloud computing
- Essentials of VMware vRealize Suite
- Designing the VMware vRealize Suite
- Designing VMware vSphere for your cloud

Cloud computing essentials

Cloud computing is a solution that provides **Computing as a Service** via a public accessible portal and offers computing resources on demand, such as desktop-to-data centers and hybrid **Desktop as a Service** (**DaaS**). The most essential characteristics of every cloud product are pay-per-use, elastic resources, self-service, and so on.

Cloud computing services are classified into three major groups:

*   IaaS
*   PaaS
*   SaaS

The following diagram illustrates a conceptual view of these services:

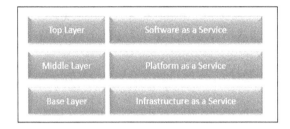

Cloud computing as a service more than a product—in other words, shared resources, software, and data—and is provided to end-user devices as a service over a network. The following diagram illustrates traditional computing components as services:

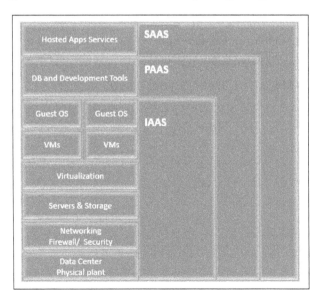

Let's get started by understanding each service. We'll begin with IaaS. It has the ability to deliver computing resources, such as a VDI, DaaS, VMs, to cloud consumers. Other essential computing systems can be delivered to consumers as well, where they can deploy guest operating systems, applications, middleware products, and databases in their comfort zone. Here, consumers can't control the underlying hardware, but they can request for information/change in it via their cloud consumer portal.

PaaS has the competence to provide resources, such as cloud infrastructure, consumer developed apps, libraries, services, and tools to other consumer. Again, the consumer can't control the underlying hardware, but they can request for information/change in it via their cloud consumer portal.

SaaS has the competence to provision applications residing on a cloud to their consumers, so they can use them from their cloud service provider. The apps should be accessible from any device that is in line with cloud security. Here, consumers cannot control the underlying hardware, but they can request for information/change in it via their cloud consumer portal.

The following table explains basic terminologies and descriptions associated with cloud computing:

Terminology	Description
Anything-as-a-Service	Anything-as-a-Service (XaaS) refers to the growing diversity of services available over a network via the cloud as on premises or off premises.
Cloud provisioning	This is the process of allocating resources on demand from the cloud.
Cloud migration	Cloud migration is a component used to transition all or part of an organization's data, apps, and services from on-premises behind a firewall of the cloud, where information can be provided over a network on demand.
Cloud service provider	A cloud service provider offers consumer storage or software solutions available via a network.
Cloud consumer	A cloud consumer is the user of a cloud-based infrastructure.
Cloud multitenant	This is a phrase used to describe multiple consumer sharing hosting layers that a public cloud provides with full isolation and security in place.

In the following section, we will discuss cloud computing deployment models.

Cloud computing helps you to build IT as a service, which is capable of transforming the power of virtualization into large computing resource pools with various cloud computing characteristics. Cloud computing can be deployed using three different cloud computing deployments models, such as **Private Cloud**, **Public Cloud**, and **Hybrid Cloud**.

The following diagram shows several diverse deployment models for the implementation of cloud technology:

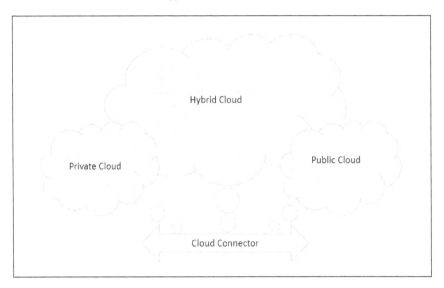

We'll now learn about each deployment model.

Public Clouds are managed by a cloud service provider that offers other enterprises or entities quick access to reasonable computing resources.

A **Private Cloud** is managed by its own company and controls its own cloud resources. **Private Clouds** exist to take the lead in numerous cloud competencies, including multitenancy capabilities.

A **Hybrid Cloud** is the integration of a **Private Cloud** with a **Public Cloud**. Actually, a **Private Cloud** can't exist in separation from other systems. Most enterprises with **Private Clouds** will change it in order to do workload crossways across cloud datacenters.

Now, let's discuss the characteristics of a cloud:

- **Self-service**: Self-service can aid cloud consumers to discretely access cloud-based IT properties, giving them the liberty to self-provision these properties. Once the setup is complete, the usage of self-provisioned IT resources can be automated, thus requiring no further involvement from a cloud provider or cloud consumer.

- **Elastic**: Elastic is the automated capability of a cloud to plainly scale IT resources on demand in response to runtime circumstances or as determined by the cloud provider or cloud consumer.

- **Metering**: This is the process of measuring the cloud usage by cloud consumers. Metering represents the historical usage of the cloud and keeps track of cloud utilization on a per user/server basis.

- **Resource pooling**: This permits cloud providers to pool large-scale IT resources to assist multiple cloud tenants. Here, dissimilar physical and virtual IT resources are dynamically allotted and redistributed in response to cloud consumer demands, which is typically followed by the implementation of services through multiplexing that is arithmetic in nature.

- **Mobility**: This is predominantly attractive for businesses so that during business hours or non-office hours, cloud consumers can stay in touch with their projects, contacts, and customers, regardless of whether they are operating from work, or are at home. A broad network entree contains Private Clouds that function within an enterprise's associated firewall.

IT as a Service (ITaaS) is a functional model where IT enterprises run much like a business, performing and functioning as a dissimilar business entity and creating products for other organizations within the enterprise.

The main advantages of a cloud are illustrated in the following diagram:

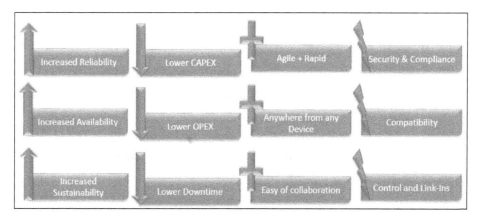

Cloud fit-for-purpose considerations

The easiest way to define *fit-for-purpose* is a cloud that offers an established solution to known problems, usually those that are a part of a larger collection. Without acknowledging this, we already used a method of applying solutions to solve known problems on a daily basis. In the world of IT, *fit-for-purpose* is the context that a cloud equates to design patterns. Let's explore the following *fit-for-purpose* concepts one by one:

- **Automated administration**: The current problem in the IT world is to manage applications, data, technology, and users who undertake frequent administrative tasks that are essential and constant; administrative problems, such as human error and slow response time, create even more of a bottleneck. For such problems, the cloud provides a more sophisticated solution. The cloud solution for this problem is to automate administration jobs that are suitable for these purposes. This is done using scripts and on a that is platform capable of running these scripts in response to predefined runtime events. The following diagram illustrates the API that performs automated administration in a cloud:

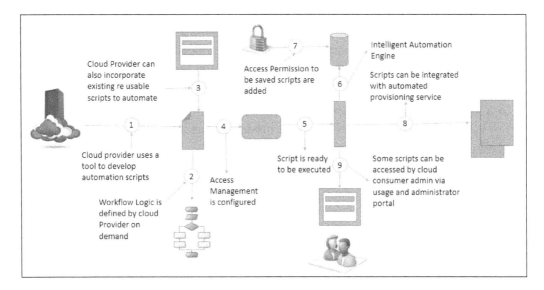

Observing the preceding diagram, it is visible that we need an API that performs an intelligent automation operation. This API should be an engine that is capable of managing, storing, and executing the automation scripts.

- **Dynamic scalability**: In the current IT world, zero dispensation management is necessary. If the request for the IT reserve is below its volume, then it is underperforming; if the request is above its volume, it is performing above its target or sometimes, the volume is unable to meet the request. To deal with this problem, the cloud provides a unified solution—the IT resource can be unified with a sensitive cloud architecture capable of automatically growing parallel or perpendicularly in response to demand. The following diagram illustrates the API's dynamic scalability in the cloud:

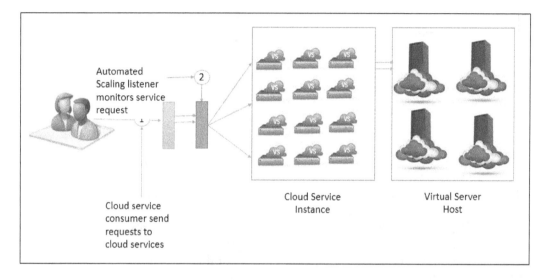

This API does the job of performing dynamic parallel scaling, which can be allowed by pooling indistinguishable IT resources and components that are capable of scattering and withdrawing workloads across each pool. Dynamic perpendicular scaling can be allowed via a technology that is capable of exchanging IT resource mechanisms at runtime.

- **Elastic resource capacity**: In the present IT scenario, the VM is underperforming and exceeding its host capacity. The cloud provides a solution for this problem as well. The elastic provisioning system actively assigns a CPU and memory for a VM in response to the changeable processing supplies of its hosted IT resources. The following diagram illustrates the API's elastic capacity in the cloud:

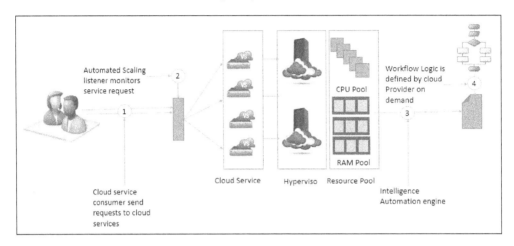

- **Self-provisioning**: As of now, in the current IT scenario, physical or semiautomated IT resource provisioning procedures make customers wait for a long time. The cloud provides a solution for this—a self-service portal that is well known and provides the ability to interface with backend structures that are required for the fully automated provisioning of IT resources. The following diagram illustrates the provisioning process in the cloud:

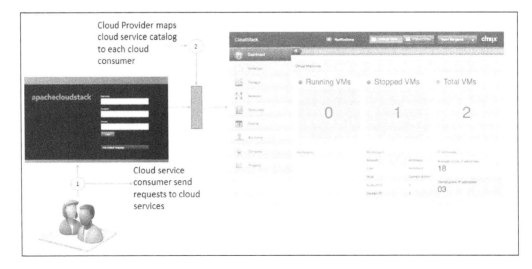

The API provides a solution in the form of frontend panels for the end users of a cloud in order to choose IT resources with fully automated provisioning capabilities. The self-service panel is also equipped with the capacity to accept a feed from the available IT resources that are accessible for provisioning.

- **Virtual server auto crash recovery**: At the time of writing this, a VM's guest OS might fail unexpectedly; it needs to be intelligent enough to have its cloud services recovered automatically. The solution for this is especially for VMs, which are continually monitored and traced for recovery in the event that a guest OS disaster occurs. The following diagram shows the auto-crash scenario in the cloud:

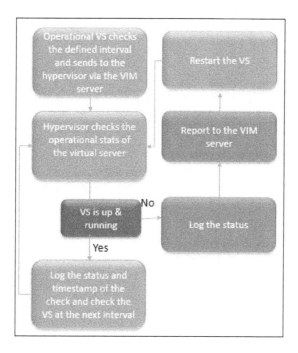

Applying this solution to an API includes applying the precise methods and mechanisms that are used by the virtualization hypervisor to check the operational status of the virtual server. The ensuing diagram illustrates the autorecovery process in the cloud:

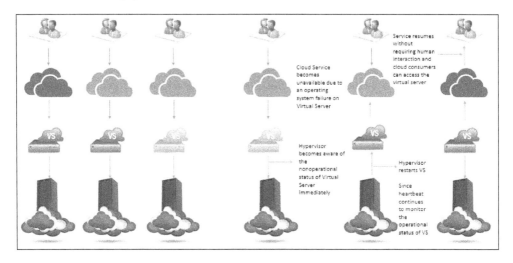

- **Pay as you go**: At the time of writing this, purchasing or leasing an entire IT source can prove to be more costly than the actual amount that the IT resource has utilized. The cloud provides a solution to this problem. It presents a system that measures the genuine IT resource consumption at a granular level and consistently bills only for the usage of that particular IT resource. The API can identify cloud usage with a runtime monitoring feature. The following diagram illustrates the pay-as-you-go facility in the cloud:

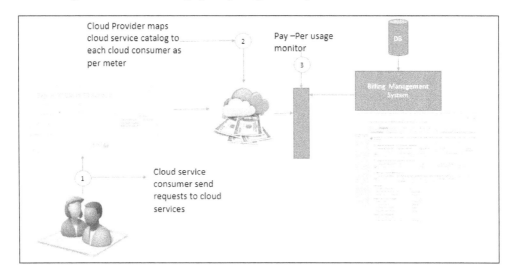

VMware vRealize Suite essentials

The **VMware vRealize Suite** is an attempt to find a management solution for data centers and the hybrid cloud. vRealize Suite combines the infrastructure and applications needed to increase business agility to provide full control over IT. vRealize Suite provides the most inclusive management stack for **Public Clouds** and **Private Clouds**. It also provides multiple virtualization hypervisors along with a physical infrastructure. It consists of the following products:

- VMware vRealize Automation Enterprise or Advanced
- VMware vRealize Log Insight
- VMware vRealize Operations Enterprise or Advanced
- VMware vRealize Business
- VMware vRealize Code Stream (not part of the suite)
- VMware vRealize Orchestrator (not part of the suite)
- VMware vRealize Hyperic (not part of the suite)

The following diagram illustrates the real-world usage of VMware vRealize on physical, virtual, and cloud infrastructures:

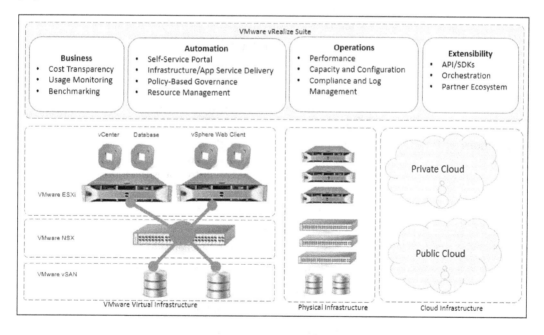

VMware vRealize offers considerable benefits in terms of quickness and cost efficiency, but cloud computing platforms are not merchandise, where one product can easily be replaced with another.

The VMware vRealize Suite delivers a platform that is built for the Hybrid Cloud and developed to automate the administration of infrastructures and applications. It provides an inclusive management stack for IT services facilitated by virtualization hypervisors, including VMware vSphere, **VMware vCloud Air**, and **Amazon Web Services**, with a unique unified management pane and the physical infrastructure.

The VMware vRealize Suite is available in two editions: VMware vRealize Suite Advanced and VMware vRealize Suite Enterprise. Now let's see how each of these products contributes to the world of the cloud. The following table illustrates their purpose:

Product	Purpose
VMware vRealize Automation	The VMware vRealize Automation product offers a secure portal where accredited administrators, developers, or IT users can demand new IT services. With this product, a user can manage both cloud and IT possessions that allow IT groups to offer services that can be systematized to their lines of business. vRealize Automation introduces the following features: <ul><li>Agility via cloud automation</li><li>Personalization via governance policies</li><li>Flexibility choices</li><li>Efficiency via cost suppression</li></ul>
VMware vRealize Operations	VMware vRealize Operations Manager 6.0 is fully integrated with VMware's integrated operations suite, uniting performance, configuration, and capacity management. This release introduces the following enhancements: <ul><li>Unified GUI and scalable implementation architecture</li><li>The choice of using Licensing Management</li><li>Nifty alerts and improved reporting</li><li>Capacity planning and custom policies</li><li>Automated remediation of snags</li><li>United Storage Visibility</li><li>UAC management</li></ul>

Product	Purpose
VMware vRealize Log Insight	This product provides a real-time log administration for the VMware infrastructure. The VMware vRealize log is created via machine-learning-based intelligent grouping, and it provides great performance. Its search operations allow faster access for management across systems and infrastructure, including the cloud. VMware vRealize Log Insight can investigate 1 TB of logs, regulate the structure of unstructured data, and deliver enterprise-wide perceptibility using a web portal. This release introduces the following enhancements: • Event trends analyzer and role-based UAC • Supports the integration of vRealize Operations Manager 6.0 • HA-combined load balancer • Built-in gratified packs and internationalization • Enhanced vRealize Log Insight Linux Agents • UI, performance, and security improvements
VMware vRealize Business	VMware vRealize Business offers transparency between the cost of cloud infrastructure and IT services. Using this, infrastructure teams can comprehend the charges of supplying private cloud and public cloud environments, with a C-level product executive comprehending the costs of providing IT services for clients. vRealize Business introduces the following features: • Bringing IT in line with business needs • Gaining clarity and forecasting TCO and ROI • Providing data facts for the CIO Transformation Agenda • Regulating and improving the IT budget

Product	Purpose
VMware vRealize Code Stream	This is an automated product that allows an enterprise to deliver quality software while using the tools in the build, test, development, staging, provisioning, and monitoring infrastructures. vRealize Code Stream introduces these features: • Offers application modeling process releases • The vRealize Automation process integrates with existing models and artifact management • Elasticity of provisioning resources and implementing engines • Provides a release console and extensibility for management • Integration of `Jenkins`
VMware vRealize Orchestrator	It simplifies the automation of multifaceted IT administration efforts. It is combined with VMware vCloud Suite components to familiarize and educate you about operational management and service delivery by successfully working with the existing environment, its gears, and processes. vRealize Orchestrator introduces these features: • Quickens process automation • A modest robust workflow automation • Open and elastic architecture • Powerful administration features • The opportunity to familiarize with and spread vRealize Automation's service delivery abilities • Automation of vRealize Operation's remedial actions
VMware vRealize Hyperic	VMware vRealize Hyperic is an element of VMware vRealize Operations. It displays real-time monitoring of the OS, middleware, and apps running in virtual, cloud, and physical infrastructures. It introduces the following features: • Monitoring the OS, application, middleware, and infrastructure • It integrates with the vRealize Operations product

The design of the VMware vRealize Suite

VMware vRealize Suite consists of these products: VMware vRealize Automation, VMware vRealize Operations, VMware vRealize Log insight, and VMware vRealize Business.

Let's get started with VMware vRealize Automation. It provides a secured web-based portal where authorized administrators, developers, and IT users can request for new IT services and manage explicit clouds. Also, it helps them ensure that there is IT compliance with the required business policies in place. Requests for IT services — including desktop, applications, infrastructure, and many others — are handled through a shared service catalog in order to offer reliable user practices.

vRealize Automation monitors cost control by revealing the cost of cloud-based resources and offering simplified resource management with reporting on resource utilization. The following diagram illustrates the services this product offers:

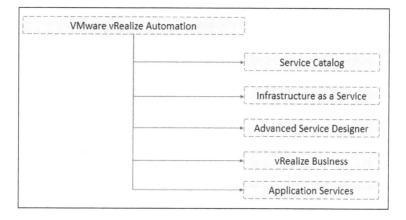

The service catalog of vRealize Automation offers a unified self-service portal to consume IT services. Cloud consumers can browse the catalog to request for items on demand, and they can track their requests and manage their own cloud-provisioned items. Cloud service architects and cloud administrators can define new services and publish them to the mutual service catalog. When defining a catalog of services, the cloud architect can agree on the components that are requested by a cloud consumer. The vRealize Automation product offers various service catalogs, as illustrated in the following diagram:

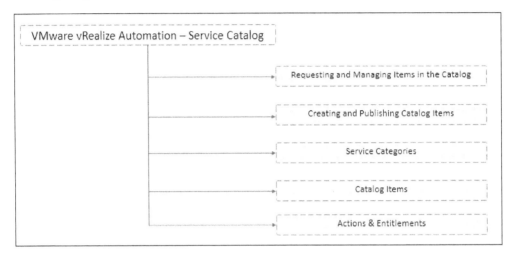

The infrastructure service offers a model to provision servers and desktops across virtual, physical, and cloud infrastructures, including private cloud, public cloud, and hybrid cloud. The VMware vRealize model works by creating a blueprint of the system, which is a description of a virtual, physical, or cloud system. Blueprints are issued as catalog items in the shared service catalog. When a user requests a system, IaaS allows us to manage the system's life cycle in line with the request. It also provisions administrative approval through decommissioning and reclamation of the resource. The vRealize Automation product offers various IaaSes that are illustrated in this diagram:

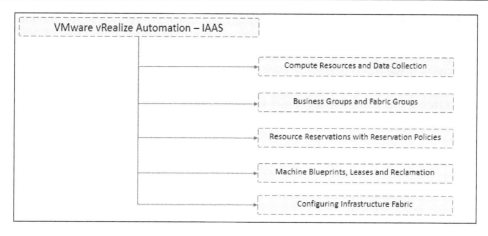

Advanced Service Designers and cloud service architects can develop advanced services and provision them as catalogs. Using these services, we can provide XaaS by employing the abilities of VMware vRealize Orchestrator. We can also create a service that allows a cloud consumer to request a backup of a database. After finishing and submitting the backup request, the cloud consumer receives a backup file of the database they specified. Using **Advanced Service Designer**, a cloud service architect can develop a custom IT source mapped to VMware vRealize Orchestrator's object types, and set them as items to be provisioned. The cloud service architect can then develop blueprints through vRealize Orchestrator workflows, and these workflows can be either fixed or independently developed by workflow developers. The vRealize Automation product offers various Advanced Service Designer functionalities, which are illustrated in the following diagram:

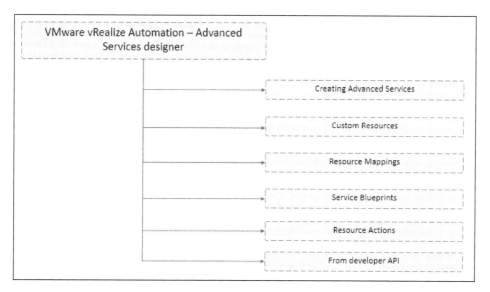

vRealize Business Standard Edition is part of the VMware vRealize suite. Directors of cloud operations can monitor their costs and design more cost-effective cloud services. The next diagram illustrates the key benefits of the vRealize business. This business drives accountability by providing reflectiveness in the cost of a public cloud and virtual infrastructure. Also, it promotes productivity in the virtual infrastructure by making it imaginable so that consumers can compare the costs, availability, and efficiency of their private cloud with the public cloud.

Application Services, formerly known as **Application Director**, helps us automate and accomplish the life cycle of multitier enterprise applications in a hybrid cloud infrastructure. A cloud consumer can regulate, configure, implement, update, and scale complex applications in a dynamic cloud infrastructure. These applications can range from simple web-based applications to complex, custom, and wrapped applications. The artifact management feature in VMware vRealize supports the use of logical names for build files and other kinds of software artifacts, allowing cloud consumers to deploy applications without considering the location.

The following diagram illustrates the features of VMware vRealize Automation's **Application Services**:

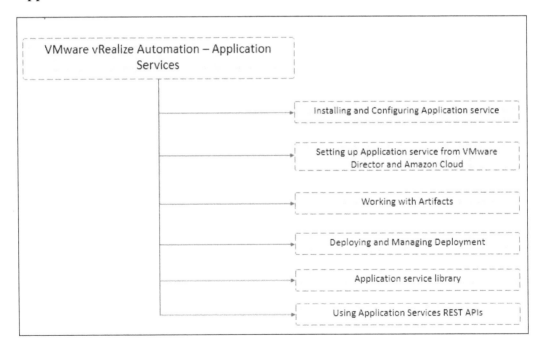

Designing VMware vSphere for your cloud

In this section, we will consider target server consolidation, the server infrastructure's resource optimization, rapid provisioning, and server standardization. This standardization will, in turn, focus on reducing the operational overhead and total cost of ownership by simplifying the administration tasks and getting rid of complex processes when designing vSphere for your cloud. The main four pillars that should be looked at are **Compute resources**, **Storage resources**, **Networking resources**, and **Security resources**.

In your design, you can express rough policies for each part of the traffic that moves across a vNIC, growing the perceptibility within virtual data center traffic while offering deviations to physical firewalls. The VMware vShield vApp allows policies to dynamically set application-level limitations instead of system-level limitations. This technique—based on resource and security protocols—allows a fast and safe method of deploying new workloads. The following is a conceptual diagram that shows how to construct a cloud based on vSphere:

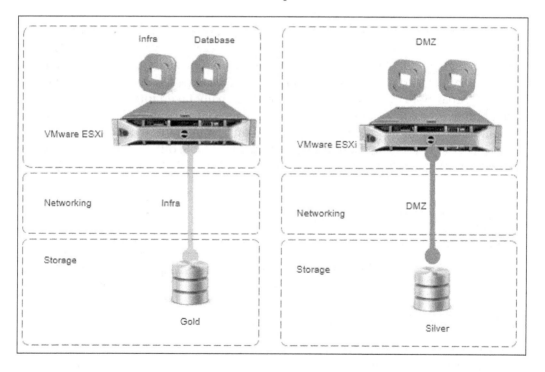

Each diverse kind of column is carved into dissimilar resource pools for all separate kinds of workload. The VM or vApp, irrespective of the kind, will be installed in any of the three resource pools. Computing and network resources, along with security pool forms, are currently well-defined and built according to what the virtual environment is capable of hosting.

Sizing and scalability play a major role in your design; in the upcoming section, we will take closer look at their core benefits. VMware strongly recommends that you use a structured block approach to computing resources for the vSphere infrastructure. By using this method, a reliable form of involvement will definitely be in place for the inner clients. By the design, we can allow both flat and perpendicular scaling on demand. It's about scalability; sizing is based on the evaluation of aspirants who wish to make use of virtualization. Consider the following key factors in your design:

- Workload estimations
- Network
- Storage

The scenario we are going to discuss now will help you identify the required parameters in your design in order to calculate the VMware ESXi host's needs. The following guideline considers growth over a 1-year period from present. This is done to regulate the essential count of VMware ESXi hosts required to combine x86 virtualization aspirants. Enhancements should be assessed and analyzed via VMware Capacity Planner. The analysis has principally taken into account source consumption for each system, including normal as well as peak CPU and memory consumption. The values should be smoothed up to make sure that acceptable resources will exist during little resource bursts. This table outlines the outcome of the CPU study:

Performance metric	Outcome
Average number of CPUs per physical system	2.1
Average CPU MHz	2,800 MHz
Average CPU utilization per physical system	12 percent (350 MHz)
Average peak CPU utilization per physical system	36 percent (1,000 MHz)
Total CPU resources of all virtual machines during peak time	202,000 MHz
Average amount of RAM per physical system	2,048 MB
Average memory utilization per physical system	52 percent (1,065 MB)
Average peak memory utilization per physical system	67 percent (1,475 MB)
Count of RAM for each VM throughout peak time (no memory sharing)	275,000 MB

Performance metric	Outcome
Assumed benefits of memory sharing when virtualized	25 percent
Count of RAM for each VM throughout peak time (memory sharing)	206,000 MB

The following tabulated recital data, collected in combination with the examination of CPU and RAM requirements, determines the high-level CPU and RAM requirements that a VMware ESXi host should provide. It illustrates the analysis of specifications required for a 1-year road map. Similarly, consider these factors of a growing organization when designing:

Factors	Specification
Allowed number of CPUs (sockets) per ESXi host	2
Allowed number of cores per CPU (AMD)	8
Allowed MHz per CPU core	2,300 MHZ
Count of CPU MHz per ESXi host	36,800 MHz
Prearranged maximum host CPU usage	80 percent
Accessible CPU MHz per ESXi host	29,400 MHz
Accessible RAM per ESXi host	76,800 MB
Count of RAM per ESXi host	96,000 MB
Prearranged maximum host RAM usage	80 percent

We don't need to calculate the minimum number of ESXi hosts from the viewpoint of both the CPU and memory. The next table will illustrate what you need to do to meet the demands:

Type	Total peak resources required	Available resources per host	ESXi hosts needed to satisfy resource requirements
CPU	202,000 MHz	29,440 MHz	7
RAM	206,000 MB	76,800 MB	3
Number of ESXi hosts required	Percentage of growth factored in	Availability requirements	Number of ESXi hosts required
7	20	N+1	10

Let's talk about network and storage now. In most cases, the network bandwidth of a VM is unnoticed and an overall hypothesis ends concerning the count of NIC vital to reach the mutual bandwidth requirements for the VM. The study has found that the typical expectable network bandwidth is 4.21 Mbps, which is completely based on a data fact across the ESXi host, which holds close to 20 VMs on it.

While designing the storage in your design, it is important to meet the I/O operations of the VM that will be placed on the storage. An I/O operation is a description of a VM's pattern. Some data objects from the software are severely exploited during reads/writes, whereas others are ruthlessly exploited on generous access, and the rest are exploited on arbitrary access. For this specific scenario, the regular I/O should be 42 IOPS for a VM.

The number of VMs to be stored per LUN can augment the sum of the forecast sizes of an application and its associated files for a VM within a VMware vSphere implementation. The following table illustrates the details of an industry study of a virtualization application across storage requirements:

Average C:\ drive size in GB	Average C:\ drive used in GB	Average X:\ drive size in GB (X means other)	Average X:\ drive used in GB (X means other)
17	10	94	41

ESXi host design and configuration considerations for a cloud

The following factors need to be considered in your host design and configuration of the cloud:

- **Domain Name Service (DNS)**: DNS must be configured for both ways: forward and reverse lookup.

- **Network Time Protocol (NTP)**: An NTP should be configured across all the ESXi hosts, and we should have NTP synchronization in place, along with VMware vCenter Server. This will help us achieve consistency across all infrastructure-virtualized servers.

- **Disk considerations**: VMware ESXi 5.5 and later versions support the following disk type for booth such as the local disk, USB/SD, SAN, and even from stateless. The majority of consumers use stateless for the purpose of saving costs and administration effort, though VMware recommends that you implement VMware ESXi on SD.

- **Installation considerations**: It is worth considering using shared volume in your design, even though VMware recommends using NFS data stores.

vCenter design essentials for the cloud

In your design, it's recommended that you implement vCenter Server on a VM. This helps the system administrator set up vCenter with HA mode. This will enable the vCenter Server VM in the event of a hardware failure, and the cloud consumer will be able to enjoy the benefits of using the cloud.

Another point to take into consideration in your design is that vCenter Server sizing should consider the growth benchmark of 20 percent for every year. Also, in your design, consider isolating the VMware vCenter Update Manager from vCenter Server during the off-maintenance period.

Cluster design essentials for the cloud

It's worth considering the design of the cluster. A collection of ESXi hosts forms a cluster in order to provide a platform for collection of VMs needing network and storage. Grouping of clustering ESXi streamline the utilization of product features, such as VMware vMotion, HA, FT DPM, and DRS. It is best to create a single cluster with all the 10 ESXi hosts. This is because, from an HA standpoint, numerous clusters will provide an outcome in the form of complex overhead.

This method can also decrease complications in your infrastructure and help elude the related effort of handling multiple substances. The following table illustrates the features that should be considered for your design:

Type	Configuration consideration
Total number of ESXi hosts	10
DRS	Should be enabled
HA	Should be enabled

This diagram illustrates vCenter for a cloud:

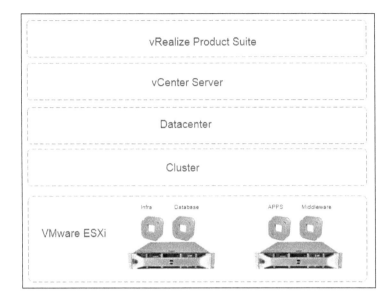

Network design essentials for the cloud

In your cloud design, you can consider the network layer as the best class to match the requirements. The network encompasses all of the network communication between the VM, ESXi, management layer, and physical network. In addition to this, you need to consider the key infrastructure potential along with networking-related aspects, such as obtainability, security, and recital.

The design of network architecture should fulfill infrastructure requirements, so here are some recommendations. Always consider:

- Separating the networks of vSphere management, VM connectivity, vMotion traffic, and NFS in your design
- Using VDS with at least two active physical adapter ports in your design
- Using redundancy at the physical switch level in your design

For simplicity and ease of management, it is recommended that you use VDS in your design. Use this in combination with manifold port groups in association with VLAN IDs to detach the ESXi host first, followed by **vMotion, VMs**, and **NFS** traffic kinds. Utilizing NetIOC should be also taken into account. This is required in order to avoid **Denial of Service (DOS)** attacks and make sure that there is fairness during times of argument. The following diagram illustrates one of the possible design consideration scenarios for networking and VDS:

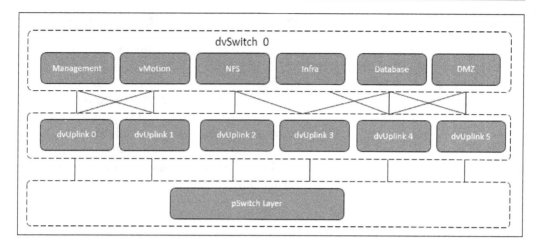

Storage design essentials for the cloud

The next important component that needs to be considered is storage. This is the most common characteristic of data store sizing—the number of VMs per data store. Data store sizing is not an easy factor, and it is exclusive to each enterprise. The next factors that should be considered are performance and availability. These, along with decreasing operational cost and effort, are the key drivers of your design.

VMware vSphere **Storage DRS (SDRS)** provides smart VM assignment, load balancing mechanisms found on I/O, and the obtainability of storage capacity. SDRS helps in drastically reducing the active cost and efforts linked with allocation of VM and monitoring the retail storage infrastructure usage. This is worth considering if you wish to implement Storage DRS.

VMware vSphere, by default, sets the SDRS latency limit to 15 ms. Based on the workload, the unlike types of disks and SLAs need to be considered. You might also need to adjust this value. When I/O high availability is set to enabled, SDRS automatically enables SIOC.

Storage DRS is enabled by default to avoid the *out-of-space* issue, since the threshold is configured at 80 percent. Thereafter, SDRS is needed if more than 80 percent of a data store is used up. SDRS will then decide whether the references' duty has to be ended, and if so, then it will decide whether they should be grounded on progress outlines, hazards, or benefits. It is worth considering the default value—always—for *out-of-space* issues in your design.

Security design essentials for the cloud

The VMware vShield App will reduce the functioning effort connected to securing the virtual environment due to its capability of smearing policies to numerous virtual mechanisms. The vShield App will set the flow of configuration to dissimilar security zones and deliver a secure virtual environment. A fresh solution created on vShield App must be implemented on every infrastructure that you purpose a design for. vShield App helps create a secured zone with associated security policies on many vCenter substances. In order to offer a secure and scalable methodology to achieve the protected infrastructure, it is best to take into account security collections based on resource pooling in your virtual infrastructure.

The following diagram illustrates usage of the vShield App in a virtual infrastructure:

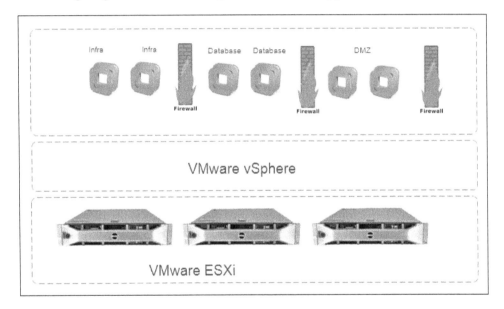

The aforementioned methodology, with secured zones based on Resource Pools, allows you to stop the certain kind of traffic between the Resource Pools that are underprivileged of the need to provide the IP addresses. All VMs from the resource pools will get the stated rules from its parent node. Every back-and-forth traffic will be obstructed, unless there is exception set. If a VM moves between resources pools, its security policy should be modified, with references to the principal resource pool policy.

It is worth considering this product in your design to create proper rules based on the real network configuration. vShield App consists of a vShield App VM and a vShield module per ESXi host.

Summary

In this chapter, you read about cloud computing essentials, fit-for-purpose concepts for the cloud, VMware vRealize Suite essentials and design, and designing VMware vSphere for your cloud. I hope that you have enjoyed reading this book. Thanks once again for choosing this book as your companion on the road to gaining knowledge of the design essentials of VMware sphere.

About VMware vSphere 6.0

vSphere 6.0 has just released. We know that VMware is a business foremost virtualization suite. VMware invests organizations to virtualize x86 servers and VDI with composed businesses, enabling functions such as availability and business continuity options in a virtualizing data center. As a result, the customer gains, on demand, an extremely resilient environment for their business to grow. In turn, this is a perfect build for any cloud environment. VMware vSphere 6.0 is a blockbuster release that encompasses new features and enhancements.

New features of VMware vSphere 6.0

vSphere 6.0 is packed with more than 650 new features and improvements that will allow customers to virtualize applications with self-assurance by scaling performance and providing breakthrough accessibility, storage productivities for VMs, and simplified management for the virtual data center. vSphere 6.0 is purpose built for both scale-up and scale-out apps, including newer big data, cloud, mobile, and social applications.

The following are some of the new features in VMware vSphere:

- **Amplified scalability**: ESXi hosts are enhanced with the following:
    - 480 CPUs
    - 12 TB of memory

  VMs are enhanced with these:
    - 128 vCPUs
    - 4 TB (vRAM)
    - 2,048 VMs per ESXi host
    - 64 nodes per cluster

- **Lingering support**: Features support for the latest model of enhanced x86-based systems and guest OS.

- **Graphics (NVIDIA GRID vGPU)**: This feature offers all the aids of NVIDIA hardware-accelerated graphics as virtualized explanations.

- **Immediate Clone**: This feature lays the basis for rapidly cloning and deploying VM. This clone deploys it as much as 10 times faster than is possible with the current version.

In the network area, enhancements such as **Network I/O Control** (**NetIOC**), Multicast Snooping, and Multiple TCP/IP Stack for vMotion are provided. They are explained here:

- **NetIOC support**: Provides support for new features, such as per-VM VDS bandwidth fixation, to ensure separation and execute the threshold in the bandwidth.

- **Multicast Snooping**: Offers support for IGMP snooping to IPv4 packet and MLD snooping for IPv6 packets in VDS. In turn, this boosts the performance and scales up with multicast traffic.

- **Multiple TCP/IP Stack for vMotion**: Provide permission for vMotion traffic to commit to the networking stack.

In the storage area, better transformations have been introduced in vSphere 6.0. By bringing in new features named **Storage Policy Based Management**, this allows mutual administration across storage layers and the dynamic storage class of offering for automation and provisioning. This gathers the particular combinations of clones, templates, and snapshots to be additionally composed per VM.

In the management area, enhancements such as the Content Library, Cross-vCenter Clone and Migration, and an enhanced UI are introduced. They are explained here:

- **Content Library**: This feature acts as a central repository that can provide easy and active administration for content management, such as managing VM templates, scripts, and ISO images. Using the vSphere Content Library, from this version, it is conceivable to keep and administer comfortabiy from a central location, and it is easy to share through publish and subscribe prototype.

- **Cross-vCenter Clone and Migration**: This is a new feature introduced in vSphere 6 that aids to copy or move VMs between ESXi hosts on disparate vCenter Servers from solitary action.

- **Enhanced User Interface**: This features enhancements introduced in vSphere 6.0 to aid the Web Client. It is better streamlined than in the previous version.

In the availability area, enhancements such as vMotion Enhancements, Replication-Assisted vMotion, and fault tolerance are built in. They are described here:

- **vMotion Enhancements**: This enhancement has been brought in to provide business with the non-disruptive live-migrating loads across VDS and vCenter Servers from a distance of up to 100 ms RTT.

- **Replication-Assisted vMotion**: This is a newer feature compared to the previous version. It empowers enterprises with active and active replication configured between two sites, and provides resource savings that are as much as 95 percent higher, depending on data size.

- **Fault Tolerance**: This feature has enhancements in vSphere 6.0 that support up to four vCPUs. These CPUs provide prolonged support for application-enabled fault tolerance for a capacity of four vCPUs.

The following table provides a comparison of features for versions of VMware vSphere:

Components	vSphere 5.5	vSphere 6.0
ESXi per cluster host	32	64
VMs per cluster	4,000	8,000
CPUs per host	320	480
RAM per host	4 TB	12 TB
VMs per host	512	2048
Virtual CPUs per VM	64	128
Virtual RAM per VM	1 TB	4 TB
FT CPU	1 vCPU	4 vCPU

Index

Symbol

4D stage analysis
Define 11
Deliver 11
Develop 11
Discover 11

A

active-active storage system
about 98
capabilities 100
Active Directory (AD) 42
active-passive storage system
about 99
capabilities 100
Advanced Service Designer 135
Amazon Web Services 130
Anything-as-a-Service (XaaS) 121
Application Architecture 24
Application Director 136
Application Services
about 136
features 136
asymmetrical storage system
about 99
capabilities 100
Asymmetric Logical Unit Access (ALUA) 99

B

bidirectional traffic shaping 71
bridge 60
Bridge Protocol Data Units (BPDU) 70
Business Architecture 24

BusLogic Parallel 92

C

cloud
cluster, design consideration 141
ESXi host configuration, considerations 140
ESXi host design, considerations 140
network, design consideration 142
security, design consideration 144
storage, design consideration 143
vCenter, design consideration 141
VMware vSphere, designing 137-139
cloud computing
about 120, 121
characteristics 123
deployment models 122
IaaS 120
PaaS 120
SaaS 120
cloud consumer 121
cloud fit-for-purpose
considerations 124-128
cloud migration 121
cloud multi-tenant 121
cloud provisioning 121
cloud service provider 121
Common Information Model (CIM) 29
community PVLAN 76
components, VMware vSphere
database 3
ESXi 2
Management layer 2
vCompute 3
vNetwork 3
vStorage 3

I/O virtualization 79
isolated PVLAN 76
IT as a Service (ITaaS) 123
IxChariot 82

J

Jumbo frames (JF) 17

L

Large Receive Offload (LRO) 17
Link Aggregation Control
        Protocol (LACP) 69
local storage 104-107
low-level design 17
LSI Logic Parallel 92
LSI Logic SAS 92

M

management layer
  about 2
  database 46
  design considerations 54
  design decisions 50
  design essentials 44
  design values 55-57
  OS instance 46
  principles 55-57
  vCenter Inventory Service 49
  vCenter SSO 48
Mean Time to Repair (MTTR) 55
multipathing
  about 110
  NAS multipathing 112, 113
  native multipathing plugin 112
  SAN multipathing 110, 111

N

NAS multipathing 112, 113
native multipathing plugin 112
NetI/O meter 82
NetQueue
  configuring 82
network
  design consideration, for cloud 142

Network Interface Controller (NIC) 60
Network I/O Control (NetIOC)
  about 17, 70, 148
  capabilities 81
Network Layer Architecture 26
Network Time Protocol (NTP) 36, 140
Network vMotion 71
NFS 142
NIC Teaming 60
NVIDIA GRID vGPU 148

O

Open Systems Interconnection (OSI)
        model 62
Open Virtualization Format (OVF)
        package 51
OS instance
  requisites 46

P

packet switching 60
path failover 110
Path Selection Plugin (PSP) 112
Physical Ethernet switch 60
physical network 60
physical switch
  selecting 73-77
Pluggable Storage Architecture (PSA) 112
Port Aggregation Protocol (PAgP) 65
port groups 64
PPP framework 5-7
primary PVLAN 76
Private Cloud 122, 129
Private Virtual Local Area Network
        (PVLAN)
  about 71, 75
  community PVLAN 76
  isolated PVLAN 76
  primary PVLAN 76
  promiscuous PVLAN 76
  secondary PVLAN 76
procedures, VMware vSphere design
  about 21
  design integration 24-26
  discovery 22

Thank you for buying
VMware vSphere Design Essentials

About Packt Publishing

Packt, pronounced 'packed', published its first book, *Mastering phpMyAdmin for Effective MySQL Management*, in April 2004, and subsequently continued to specialize in publishing highly focused books on specific technologies and solutions.

Our books and publications share the experiences of your fellow IT professionals in adapting and customizing today's systems, applications, and frameworks. Our solution-based books give you the knowledge and power to customize the software and technologies you're using to get the job done. Packt books are more specific and less general than the IT books you have seen in the past. Our unique business model allows us to bring you more focused information, giving you more of what you need to know, and less of what you don't.

Packt is a modern yet unique publishing company that focuses on producing quality, cutting-edge books for communities of developers, administrators, and newbies alike. For more information, please visit our website at www.packtpub.com.

About Packt Enterprise

In 2010, Packt launched two new brands, Packt Enterprise and Packt Open Source, in order to continue its focus on specialization. This book is part of the Packt Enterprise brand, home to books published on enterprise software – software created by major vendors, including (but not limited to) IBM, Microsoft, and Oracle, often for use in other corporations. Its titles will offer information relevant to a range of users of this software, including administrators, developers, architects, and end users.

Writing for Packt

We welcome all inquiries from people who are interested in authoring. Book proposals should be sent to author@packtpub.com. If your book idea is still at an early stage and you would like to discuss it first before writing a formal book proposal, then please contact us; one of our commissioning editors will get in touch with you.

We're not just looking for published authors; if you have strong technical skills but no writing experience, our experienced editors can help you develop a writing career, or simply get some additional reward for your expertise.

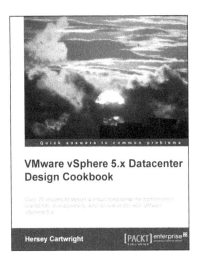

VMware vSphere 5.x Datacenter Design Cookbook

ISBN: 978-1-78217-700-5   Paperback: 260 pages

Over 70 recipes to design a virtual datacenter for performance, availability, manageability and recoverability with VMware vSphere 5.x

1. Innovative recipes, offering numerous practical solutions when designing virtualized datacenters.

2. Identify the design factors — requirements, assumptions, constraints, and risks — by conducting stakeholder interviews and performing technical assessments.

3. Increase and guarantee performance, availability, and workload efficiency with practical steps and design considerations.

VMware vSphere 5.1 Cookbook

ISBN: 978-1-84968-402-6   Paperback: 466 pages

Over 130 task-oriented recipes to install, configure, and manage various vSphere 5.1 components

1. Install and configure vSphere 5.1 core components.

2. Learn important aspects of vSphere such as administration, security, and performance.

3. Configure vSphere Management Assistant(VMA) to run commands/scripts without the need to authenticate every attempt.

Please check **www.PacktPub.com** for information on our titles

VMware vSphere 5.5 Cookbook

ISBN: 978-1-78217-285-7   Paperback: 560 pages

A task-oriented guide with over 150 practical recipes to install, configure, and manage VMware vSphere components

1. Explore the use of command line interface (CLI) to consistently configure the environment and automate it reasonably.

2. Discover the best practices to deploy stateless and statefull ESXi hosts and upgrade them.

3. Simplified and to-the-point theory to manage vSphere Storage and Networking Environment.

vSphere High Performance Cookbook

ISBN: 978-1-78217-000-6   Paperback: 240 pages

Over 60 recipes to help you improve vSphere performance and solve problems before they arise

1. Troubleshoot real-world vSphere performance issues and identify their root causes.

2. Design and configure CPU, memory, networking, and storage for better and more reliable performance.

3. Comprehensive coverage of performance issues and solutions including vCenter Server design and virtual machine and application tuning.

Please check **www.PacktPub.com** for information on our titles

www.ingramcontent.com/pod-product-compliance
Lightning Source LLC
Chambersburg PA
CBHW060136060326
40690CB00018B/3898